Who May Dwell on Your Holy Hill?

Glory Cumbow

Parson's Porch Books

www.parsonsporchbooks.com

Who May Dwell on Your Holy Hill?

ISBN: Softcover 978-1-949888-77-5

Copyright © 2019 by Glory Cumbow

All rights reserved. No part of this book may be reproduced or transmitted in any form or by any means, electronic or mechanical, including photocopying, recording, or by any information storage and retrieval system, without permission in writing from the publisher.

Contents

Introduction to Sermons Matter Series 5
Creator and the Creative 7
    Genesis 1:1-2:4a
Mother of All Living 13
    Genesis 3:16-21
Messy Relationships 17
    Genesis 45:3-11, 15
Persist, Advocate, Be Thankful 23
    1 Samuel 1:4-20
Approaching Grace with Boldness 30
    Job 23:1-9, 16-17
Who May Dwell on Your Holy Hill? 37
    Psalm 15
Longing for God 43
    Psalm 42
The Light We've Been Given 50
    Psalm 50:1-6
Labor for What Satisfies 56
    Isaiah 55:1-9
Perceived Complexity 61
    Isaiah 58:1-12
Return 68
    Joel 2:1-2, 12-17

A Conversation Between Malachi and Paul..............................73
   Malachi 3:1-4; 1 Corinthians 13:1-3, 11-13

A Story from Mary 79
   Matthew 2:13-23

Jesus Abandoned 85
   Matthew 27:45-56

Perplexed and Pondering...89
   Luke 1:26-38

Is it Real?...95
   John 1:1-5

Empty-Tomb People... 100
   John 20:19-31

Children and Heirs... 106
   Romans 8:12-25

Unity at the Table 113
   1 Corinthians 11:17-28

A Prayer to Share.. 118
   Ephesians 3:14-21

Gentleness Born of Wisdom... 124
   James 3:5-13

Now and Yet 130
   1 John 3:1-7

Introduction to Sermons Matter Series

Parson's Porch Books is delighted to present to you this series called Sermons Matter.

We believe that many of the best writers are pastors who take the role of preacher seriously. Week in, and week out, they exegete scripture, research material, write and deliver sermons in the context of the life of their particular congregation in their given community.

We further believe that sermons are extensions of Holy Scripture which need to be published beyond the manuscripts which are written for delivery each Sunday. Books serve as a vehicle for the sermon to continue to proclaim the Good News of the Morning to a broader audience.

We celebrate the wonderful occasion of the preaching event in Christian worship when the Pastor speaks, the People listen and the Work of the Church proceeds.

Take, Read, and Heed.

David Russell Tullock, M.Div., D.Min.

Publisher
Parson's Porch Books

Creator and the Creative
Genesis 1:1-2:4a

While I read the scripture passage, take a moment to close your eyes and just hear the word proclaimed to you. While you're listening, work your ball of Play-Doh back and forth in your hands. Pay attention to any images that stick out to you in the scripture or any images that come to mind as I am reading.

Genesis 1:1-2:4a

In the beginning when God created the heavens and the earth. The earth was a formless void and darkness covered the face of the deep, while a wind from God swept over the face of the waters. Then God said, "Let there be light"; and there was light. And God saw that the light was good; and God separated the light from the darkness. God called the light Day, and the darkness he called Night. And there was evening and there was morning, the first day. And God said, "Let there be a dome in the midst of the waters, and let it separate the waters from the waters." So God made the dome and separated the waters that were under the dome from the waters that were above the dome. And it was so. God called the dome Sky... And God said, "Let the waters bring forth swarms of living creatures, and let birds fly above the earth across the dome of the sky." So God created the great sea monsters and every living creature that moves, of every kind, with which the waters swarm, and every winged bird of every kind. And God saw that it was good. God blessed them, saying, "Be fruitful and multiply and fill the waters in the seas, and let birds multiply on the earth." And there was evening and there was morning, the fifth day. And God said, "Let the earth bring forth living creatures of every kind: cattle and creeping things and wild animals of the earth of every kind." And it was so. God made the wild animals of the earth of every kind, and the cattle of every kind, and everything that creeps upon the ground of every kind. And God saw that it was good. Then God said,

"Let us make humankind in our image, according to our likeness; and let them have dominion over the fish of the sea, and over the birds of the air, and over the cattle, and over all the wild animals of the earth, and over every creeping thing that creeps upon the earth." So God created humankind in his image, in the image of God he created them; male and female he created them...

If you haven't already, you may open your eyes. As you hear the words spoken over you this morning, continue working with your Play-Doh. Whatever image came to mind when you were listening to the scripture, I ask that you start forming with the dough. Take your time. If you feel like you've messed up, then start over and try again. When you're done just hang on to your sculpture. You'll need it later. I realize that this may be fun and exciting for some. Creating images and working with clay may be something that some of us enjoy. For others it may be daunting. The thought may arise that this is a difficult or frustrating task. Or maybe there might be some worry about judging one another's sculptures and comparing them with each other. There's no need to worry about competition because we're celebrating all of our gifts. What we learn from this scripture is that, by the grace of God, we are the created who are all capable of creativity.

I love that the whole of scripture begins with God's creativity, crafting us as an artwork. It's important to note that God, the grand master artist of the cosmos, begins creation with simplicity: light, dark, land, water, dome. Creation begins simply, and it is good. Then God moves to more complicated matters: vegetation, creeping things, sea monsters, and winged birds. They are good. Then came humankind, one of the most intricate and complex designs within the masterpiece, blessed among all of creation to be made in God's image. We are good.

We were given dominion over the earth, called to be participators in this on-going, ever-growing, living artwork. And I believe that if we are all created in God's image, then we are all given God's ability to create.

Often the word "creativity" is associated with the variety of artists in the world: painters, poets, actors, singers, musicians, sculptors, and so on. Artistic ability is truly a gift of the Holy Spirit, and what makes an artist successful is their passion and practice. Just as God moved from simplicity to complexity, artists must follow the same pattern in order to polish their craft. Sometimes we dodge art and creativity because we feel as if our gifts do not involve performing monologues in front of crowds or chiseling life-sized, marble sculptures. Often, we compare our abilities with the gifts of others, and we can become intimidated when we see their talents. This can cause us to doubt our creative ability because it looks different than someone else's ability. Sometimes we focus too much on the imperfections of the things we produce. We are all truly artists in this world, given gifts to contribute to creation. Any artist will tell you that often times art is far from perfect and is actually a series of "happy accidents." Instead of holding ourselves to impossible standards of comparison and perfection, we are empowered to accept that our imaginations and abilities vary from individual to individual. We are encouraged to embrace our imaginative diversity because we need creative ways to share love, spread peace, and seek justice in God's ever-changing kingdom.

Embracing our gifts means working past this compulsion to compare ourselves to others and doubt our abilities, so that we may engage our creativity. Author Madeleine L'Engle says in her book, *Walking on Water,* that we can accomplish this work by getting out of own way to become a servant to our work and listening to the inspiration that comes from the Holy Spirit. She says, "When the artist is truly the servant of the work, the work is better than the artist; Shakespeare knew how to listen to his work, and so he often wrote better than he could write; Bach composed more deeply, more truly, than he knew; Rembrandt's brush put more of the human spirit on canvas than Rembrandt could comprehend. When the work takes over, then the artist is enabled to get out of the way." She says that we must allow our work to take over so that we may hear the voice of God. Let us remember that our creative work is as diverse as we are. We create homes, families, and the little lives of children. We create work environments that are ethical. We create communities that are inclusive and just. We create schools that educate and inspire. We create hospitals that heal and soothe. As people grow and change, their needs change, and being imaginative in our work is essential to meeting people where they are. The Holy Spirit will guide us as we participate in our work, our art, as we resist comparing ourselves to one another and striving for perfection. God does not require perfection but does require faithfulness.

Perhaps another reason why so many of us keep creativity at arm's length is because it requires us to give away a piece of ourselves. In fact, God did the very same thing in creation: "So God created humankind in his image, in the image of God he created them; male and female he created them." God put God's self into the art and created us. This is the ultimate vulnerability: to expose ourselves in the things we make and give it away. But that is what Christ has called us to do in order to participate in God's kingdom: to be willing to give ourselves away; to give up everything that holds us back and fully commit to God's kingdom work. To expose our souls by imaginatively serving God with our gifts and talents could possibly bring about pain and betrayal, but it is also what shines love into the world and draws others in. In his book *Drops Like Stars,* Rob Bell talks about how we as people want to know we're not alone in our life experiences. He says that great artists and great people creatively express themselves to let others know that they are not alone. Rob Bell specifically talks about African-American spirituals and how the sorrow in the lyrics moves us. He says, "[take the song] *Sometimes I Feel like a Motherless Child,* which starts by repeating that line three times and then the line, 'a long way from home.' Like me, you've probably never been owned by someone else as a slave. And yet when we hear a song like, *Sometimes I Feel like a Motherless Child* we connect with it at some primal level of the soul-even if we've known our mothers our whole lives. We're drawn to it..." Rob Bell explains that sharing what's in our souls connects us to others. It's a risk to expose who we are to the core, but loving is risky business. God's perfect creation was destroyed by sin, a risk God took in order to create life. But God keeps drawing us in, and we are called to participate in that work.

Now I would like for everyone to hold up their Play-Doh sculptures. Take a moment and look around at each other's handiwork. Every piece of art is unique and reflective of the individual's creativity. Each one of you is capable of creativity. You are all artists in God's living masterpiece. You may put down your Play-Doh, but please don't destroy the sculptures! When the service is over, I would like you to place them on the table in the back so that we can see what all of our creation looks like when it's put together. Each one of you listened to the word of God today and created something from it. You were willing to be a servant to the work. You were willing to put a piece of yourself, your imagination, into the art and share it with those around you. This is what God asks of us: to have dominion over the earth, to be participators in God's creation. When we imagine, create, and share our own gifts, we draw others in. Let us engage in our God-given creative ability to use the gifts and skills that the Holy Spirit has given us to invite others into the reconciliation of the kingdom. Our creative work in the world might look different than our friends' and families' work. That's exactly how God crafted our abilities, no need for comparison or perfection! We may have to move slowly, beginning with simplicity before we can reach complexity. God modeled that for us, so there is no fear in taking our time, trying, failing, learning, and starting over. When God created us, we were called "good." Beloved, rest assured that our creations, when done with the love of God, is also "good."

Mother of All Living
Genesis 3:16-21

To the woman he said, "I will greatly increase your pangs in childbearing; in pain you shall bring forth children, yet your desire shall be for your husband, and he shall rule over you." And to the man he said, "Because you have listened to the voice of your wife, and have eaten of the tree about which I commanded you, 'You shall not eat of it,' cursed is the ground because of you; in toil you shall eat of it all the days of your life; thorns and thistles it shall bring forth for you; and you shall eat the plants of the field. By the sweat of your face you shall eat bread until you return to the ground, for out of it you were taken; you are dust, and to dust you shall return." The man named his wife Eve, because she was the mother of all living. And the Lord God made garments of skins for the man and for his wife and clothed them.

Today our sermon will be told from the voice of Eve. Listen to Eve's words to hear a word from God:

Please, remember my name: Mother of All Living. That includes you, dear one. I know you're probably quite angry with me. I have had many millennia of blame placed upon my shoulders for the pain and suffering in the world. I understand; I disobeyed. I made a bad choice that turned me away from God's will and disrupted the perfection of God's creation. I instigated sin. Now the world churns under the weight of my choice. You've been betrayed by others, haven't you? You've lost loved ones? You've experienced unspeakable tragedy? Those are the consequences of sin that I brought into the world. I have heard over and over again from people who think back to the moment that I ate from the fruit and they say, "Eve cursed us!" It's true. I did. However, history has shown us that it's easier to blame women for their wrongs than to credit them for their successes and contributions. I asked you to remember my name so that you knew who you came from. I also ask that you see the entire picture and examine all the details of the story. You see, I didn't sin alone. Adam was there with me too. We were supposed to care for one another and protect each other; instead we failed at our commitment to ensure the best for one another. We were a team, we were in it all together. We lived in the garden as a team, and we sinned as a team. It wasn't until both of us had eaten of the fruit that our eyes were opened and that the knowledge of good and evil had taken effect. I did not do this alone, so the blame doesn't fall only to me.

You see, Adam is the quiet, contemplative type. I love that about him. He carefully considered what God would tell him when we all walked in the garden together, and he listens intently when I share my thoughts with him. He loves to learn and ponder. So, when the crafty serpent slithered forward to tempt us into eating the fruit, Adam remained silent by my side. My approach is different. I speak boldly, willing to debate. I enjoy spirited conversations and quick wit. When the serpent questioned us about God's commands regarding the fruit of the tree, I was willing to argue back. I quipped to the creature saying that we were not allowed to eat of the fruit of the trees within the garden. I considered myself quite the theologian, but I wasn't prepared for the serpent's new tactic; this creeping, crawling animal made me doubt God's intentions. The serpent said that the fruit was not deadly as God had said. Instead this fruit would make us like God knowing good and evil. We were intrigued. Adam and I were always hungry for knowledge, and this made us hungry for the fruit. I reached up high, plucked the fruit, I ate, and I shared with Adam. He did not deny the fruit but partook with me. We fell into deception together.

Sin was already showing itself to threaten what was good in our lives. Adam and I were overcome with the feeling of exposure, vulnerability, and shame; so, we hid and covered ourselves as God came walking through the garden. And then came the first betrayal brought on by sin: Adam spoke to God to answer for our actions but blamed me instead of taking responsibility for his complicity. He said God had given him this woman and it was her fault! What a sharp pain to my heart! I'm not the deceptive serpent; we were both deceived. I was so hurt and so scared that when God asked me what happened I blamed the trickery of the serpent, also attempting to divert my own responsibility. I had never felt alone until right now in this moment. But God punished us both for what we had done. Regardless of Adam's betrayal, he was going to be punished too. There was no mercy for the serpent either. The serpent was now cursed to be the lowest creature of the earth and to be at the mercy of humanity's stomping feet.

I couldn't look at Adam. He was ashamed and couldn't look at me either. Was all lost? Was everything good between us and around us ruined? We knew we had lost our privileges to the garden, and it looked like we would lose each other too. But Adam chose the heal the rift between us. He named me. I was no longer just "woman," but Eve, Mother of All Living. He acknowledged my identity. This name is specific and unique to who I am as a person. It is important to note that the first man on earth found it important to name a woman. So many of my daughters who came after me are remembered without names. My story is just the first of many other stories to come of God's working in the world. There are stories of wandering in the wilderness, judges, kings, and prophets. So many women go unmentioned, and the few that are recognized are often times unnamed. The presence of women matters to God's story, and our names distinguish our uniqueness of being made in God's image. It's a tragedy that so many of my daughters are ignored and unnamed in the telling of the ancient stories. But Adam set the precedent by naming me, recognizing my humanity and importance to God's world.

So, we left the garden together, our relationship mended. We knew that we needed each other so that we could get through this transition from the garden to the harsher conditions of the outside world. I know you are all still suffering the consequences of our choices. I'm so sorry. If we could take it back, we would. But God only allows us to move forward in our time, so that's what we had to do. Do know that we have paid dearly: we lost our home, and I was the first mother to ever lose a child. We were the first to know the searing pain of murder. But I was also the first woman to know what it's like to build a life with her spouse, to create a family, and to make a home. Adam and I created a life together, we dreamed together, we grew together, and we loved together. In this severe world where we are all suffering under the consequences of sin, there is still goodness and joy. Although we made the gravest of errors together, we were not powerful enough to destroy the goodness of God's creation. While I understand your resentment, I humbly ask for some empathy. Without the benefit of hindsight, would you have fared any better under deception than I did? It is easy to look back and to judge the bad choices I made while neglecting what I have accomplished. Because of *my* perseverance, *you* are here today. Please, remember my name: Mother of All Living. That includes you, dear one.

Messy Relationships
Genesis 45:3-11, 15

Joseph said to his brothers, "I am Joseph. Is my father still alive?" But his brothers could not answer him, so dismayed were they at his presence. Then Joseph said to his brothers, "Come closer to me." And they came closer. He said, "I am your brother, Joseph, whom you sold into Egypt. And now do not be distressed, or angry with yourselves, because you sold me here; for God sent me before you to preserve life. For the famine has been in the land these two years; and there are five more years in which there will be neither plowing nor harvest. God sent me before you to preserve for you a remnant on earth, and to keep alive for you many survivors. So it was not you who sent me here, but God; he has made me a father to Pharaoh, and lord of all his house and ruler over all the land of Egypt. Hurry and go up to my father and say to him, Thus says your son Joseph, God has made me lord of all Egypt; come down to me, do not delay. You shall settle in the land of Goshen, and you shall be near me, you and your children and your children's children, as well as your flocks, your herds, and all that you have. I will provide for you there—since there are five more years of famine to come—so that you and your household, and all that you have, will not come to poverty.' And he kissed all his brothers and wept upon them; and after that his brothers talked with him.

In his book *The Price of the Ticket* author and civil rights activist James Baldwin says, "You think your pain and your heartbreak are unprecedented in the history of the world, but then you read. It was books that taught me that the things that tormented me most were the very things that connected me with all the people who were alive, who had ever been alive." As a man who faced discrimination for his race and sexual orientation during the civil rights era, James Baldwin knew pain. He knew the brokenness of human relationships that led to discrimination, and he knew what it meant to be treated as less than a person. He used his platform as a writer and a professor to fight for equality by digging openly and honestly into the messy, complicated issues that we as society face. While James Baldwin eventually left the Christian faith, he still kept to the message that we as the church know to be true: we are a broken people who have broken relationships with one another. We know we are a sinful people; our sinful choices that point us away from God's will of goodness, peace, truth, and love causes rifts between us and the people that we love. However, we also humble ourselves and confess these sins every Sunday together. We know that God forgives and restores us when we seek reconciliation with God and the people around us. Our messy relationships are a fact of life, but if we turn to God in humility, forgive others, and seek reconciliation then God's peace can prevail.

As we see in this scripture passage, Joseph and his brothers have complicated feelings toward one another because of their messy, broken relationship. Joseph had been arrogant about his status as the favored brother and bragged about the dreams he had that one day his brothers would bow down to him. The brothers had been so jealous that they had become murderous; their bloodlust was satisfied by selling Joseph into slavery, which was only marginally better than killing him. After years of being separated and Joseph suffering from imprisonment due to false accusations, Joseph had risen to power over Egypt at the side of Pharaoh. A famine had overtaken the land, and Joseph's brothers had travelled to Egypt to buy rations of grain. Joseph had the opportunity to use his power to accuse his brothers of their crimes and withhold grain from them; instead he hugged them, and they wept together. Joseph had decades to sit with the pain and anger at the betrayal from his family. Instead of holding onto grudges he chose to see God at work in his life to help save people from the coming famine.

Instead of adding to the brokenness, he chose to embrace the messiness of the relationship with his brothers by humbling himself, forgiving them, and reconciling with them together. Their family was able to be reunited and made whole again in Egypt; there might have still been tension and pain, but they were able to come together and move forward.

Humility is the starting point for peace. Humility doesn't mean sacrificing self-worth for the sake of keeping the peace; when someone's self-worth is treated as unimportant in a relationship, then that is abuse. Abusive parents or spouses or friends are people who manipulate others into thinking that their self-worth is not important, and that they are only as valuable as the abuser says they are. This can be manifested physically, verbally, emotionally, and sexually. We cannot let abusers steal our value; all people are valuable, important, and worthy of love. And true humility recognizes this. Humility means taking responsibility for wrongs done and recognizing that the needs and wants of yourself, and those that you love, deserve to be honored and respected. In her book, *Letter to My Daughter,* Maya Angelou describes a time when she travelled to Senegal to visit a friend and learned a lesson in humility. Her friend was throwing a dinner party and her home was beautifully decorated with many guests visiting and enjoying each other's company. In the middle of the room was a gorgeous, expensive rug that everyone was avoiding stepping on. Maya assumed that her friend had told her guests not to step on the rug, and she wanted to challenge this notion because she believed that rugs were meant to be stepped on. So, she went around the room looking at paintings and socializing, while intentionally stepping on the rug several times. As she began conversing with someone at the party, she noticed two maids who came into the room, rolled up the rug and laid out a new one with silverware, dishes, and food. Then everyone was invited to sit down at it and eat. This had not been a rug at all, but a tablecloth. Maya realized her mistake and felt deeply embarrassed for her assumptions of another culture. She is quoted to say, "In an unfamiliar culture, it is wise to offer no innovations, no suggestions or lessons. The epitome of sophistication is utter simplicity." Maya did not have to set aside her value and self-worth in learning humility, but she did have to take some time to open her eyes to the value of the traditions and culture of the people around her. Joseph went from being the favored son, to being enslaved and imprisoned. He learned a hard lesson in humility, but this allowed God to use him to save the people in the land from famine and allowed him to be able to reunite with his family.

Following a lesson in humility comes a lesson in forgiveness. It seems like we, as people and as the church, really struggle with forgiveness because when we are hurt or wronged, we want the person to receive justice. We want them to admit their wrongs and then pay for it. We want them to get on their knees and offer a sobbing apology. If none of that happens, and we all know that in reality it often doesn't happen, then we hold onto the anger towards them as if it punishes them. Again, this is not reality. We are punishing ourselves when we let our rage burn. Forgiveness does not mean we excuse a wrong done toward us, and it doesn't mean what they've done is okay. It means that we are refusing to allow the bitterness to erode all the goodness that God has placed in our soul. It means that we are trusting God with our pain and rage and allowing our souls to reflect the forgiveness that God has extended to all of us through Jesus Christ. When we forgive, we can heal.

Author Jen Hatmaker writes in her book *Of Mess and Moxie* of a time when her life erupted in pain and anger. Her friends and her church turned against her and her family, and they lost many of their friends. Months, even years later Jen found herself having pretend arguments out loud with the people that she held grudges against, practicing in the mirror so that if she ever encountered them again, she would make them feel the wrath of the pain that they had caused her. She would go over old conversations in her head, re-read emails from people who'd hurt her, and just re-open the same old wounds over and over again. One day she decided that she couldn't remain this bitter and this miserable anymore. So, Jen decided to pray for her enemies just like Jesus wanted us to do. After months of praying for these people, she found that her rage was gone and that she was healing. She had finally forgiven the people who hurt her. She hadn't forgotten the pain, because there really is no such thing as forgiving and forgetting; but she had allowed her wounds to be healed so that she could finally move on in her life and find peace. Jen was making room for God's peace in her heart, like Joseph. He was able to make room for peace by forgiving his brothers and telling them not to be angry over the past anymore.

Joseph was able to reconcile with his family. They were able to reunite in Egypt and live through the rest as their days together restored to one another. In Madeleine L'Engle's novel, *A Wind in the Door*, a fourteen-year-old girl named Meg must save her brother, Charles Wallace, from an evil force that is making him deathly ill. She must shrink down and go inside his body to fight off the evil that is infecting him, but she doesn't go on this journey alone. Meg must go with the school principal, Mr. Jenkins, who she detests. She doesn't like Mr. Jenkins because he hasn't stopped the bullies who beat up her little brother. However, the evil in her brother's body feeds on the anger and the tension between the two. Meg must find empathy for Mr. Jenkins and see him as a valuable human being before they can work together to save Charles Wallace. Mr. Jenkins risks his life to save Meg's brother, and this helps her to forgive him. Once the two reconcile their differences, Charles Wallace is saved. This type of reconciliation is the ideal: when we are able to heal from our hurts, repair our relationships, and be at peace with one another. This is a possibility in many circumstances when we humble ourselves and forgive each other; but in some circumstances this is impossible. People who are abused should never be required by anyone to go back and live with their abuser. Some people are rejected by their families for marrying someone they don't approve of or refusing to go into the family business. In many of those cases, the family remains estranged. In our broken relationships, sometimes even when we do the very best that we can our relationships can't, and maybe shouldn't, go back to the way they were before. This is the harsh reality of our messy relationships. When this happens, we try to find reconciliation with ourselves and with God, trusting in the hope that God's perfect justice and reconciliation will restore the relationships that we cannot heal in this lifetime. God can make us whole in and of ourselves.

Joseph's story is a messy one: his parents choose favorites, he shoots off at the mouth, his brothers want to murder him, then they sell him into slavery instead, he's falsely accused and imprisoned, and then he rises to power alongside of Pharaoh. In all of this God was working to save the people from starvation and to heal the broken relationships in Joseph's family. Whatever situations we might be facing, whoever has hurt us, whatever fight we find ourselves in, this pain and anger doesn't have to define us. We can learn right along with Joseph that humility, forgiveness, and reconciliation help us embrace and heal the messy relationships that we inevitably find ourselves engaged in. Also, like Joseph, may we trust that the Holy Spirit is at work in our lives, so that we might know that we do not face our hardships alone.

Persist, Advocate, Be Thankful
1 Samuel 1:4-20

On the day when Elkanah sacrificed, he would give portions to his wife Peninnah and to all her sons and daughters; but to Hannah he gave a double portion, because he loved her, though the LORD had closed her womb. Her rival used to provoke her severely, to irritate her, because the LORD had closed her womb. So it went on year by year; as often as she went up to the house of the LORD, she used to provoke her. Therefore Hannah wept and would not eat. Her husband Elkanah said to her, "Hannah, why do you weep? Why do you not eat? Why is your heart sad? Am I not more to you than ten sons?" After they had eaten and drunk at Shiloh, Hannah rose and presented herself before the LORD. Now Eli the priest was sitting on the seat beside the doorpost of the temple of the LORD. She was deeply distressed and prayed to the LORD, and wept bitterly. She made this vow: "O LORD of hosts, if only you will look on the misery of your servant, and remember me, and not forget your servant, but will give to your servant a male child, then I will set him before you as a nazirite until the day of his death. He shall drink neither wine nor intoxicants, and no razor shall touch his head." As she continued praying before the LORD, Eli observed her mouth. Hannah was praying silently; only her lips moved, but her voice was not heard; therefore Eli thought she was drunk. So Eli said to her, "How long will you make a drunken spectacle of yourself? Put away your wine." But Hannah answered, "No, my lord, I am a woman deeply troubled; I have drunk neither wine nor strong drink, but I have been pouring out my soul before the LORD. Do not regard your servant as a worthless woman, for I have been speaking out of my great anxiety and vexation all this time." Then Eli answered, "Go in peace; the God of Israel grant the petition you have made to him." And she said, "Let your servant find favor in your sight." Then the woman went to her quarters, ate and drank with her husband, and her countenance was sad no longer. They rose early in the morning and worshiped before the LORD; then they went back to their house at Ramah. Elkanah knew his wife Hannah, and the LORD remembered her. In due time Hannah conceived and bore a son. She named him Samuel, for she said, "I have asked him of the LORD."

As we prepare our homes, our food, and our travel plans for Thanksgiving, we think about all the things we are thankful for in our lives. While Thanksgiving can be a joyful holiday, it has become increasingly clear that not everyone has cause for joy. Some people are mourning lost loved ones, some are estranged from their family, and some people don't have the food and shelter to celebrate with. For those who are struggling this year, your pain and your story matters too. I see you. You are loved by this church and by our God. As we prepare for the holiday, I invite us, as the Body of Christ, to take a look at this scripture passage that navigates the complicated path to thankfulness. I believe that this story of Hannah shows us how to respond faithfully to people in all walks of life, while also providing space for joy and celebration. For those who are struggling, this story teaches how to *persist* in our needs and desires. It teaches us that it's okay not to be okay all the time, and that we have a right to ask for help from others. For those who have an abundance of blessings, this scripture passage teaches us to *advocate* with others and to be helpers to those in need. Finally, it teaches all of us to *give thanks* for what we have, because God is good.

I love this story of Hannah praying for a child. Hannah is not afraid to go after what she wants and bravely kneels before God in the temple to plead her case and implore God for her deepest desire. Hannah is a persistent woman. Instead of giving into her rival who provoked her, she continued to pursue her desire to become a mother. She persists further when Eli, the priest in the temple, tells her to stop making a drunken spectacle of herself. She stands up for herself, saying that she is not drunk at all and that she shouldn't be counted as a "worthless woman." Instead she insists that her voice matters, she is pouring out her soul and speaking her anxiety and vexation. Hannah is speaking her truth, and she refuses to be silent. I love Hannah, a strong woman who knows what she wants, who is willing to go after it, and refuses to let anyone silence her, including Eli the priest.

The best examples of persistence I have ever seen was when I spent time as a chaplain at the Outreach and Advocacy Center, or the OAC, at Central Presbyterian Church in downtown Atlanta. At the OAC my job was to do intake with people who needed to get their Georgia identity cards and their birth certificates. We also provided vouchers for food, clothing, and medical services. Most of our guests who received services at the OAC were experiencing homelessness in some shape or form. One job in particular that I loved to do was mentoring our guests who were in our program that helped people get ready for jobs. One of the OAC employees would hold free classes to help any guest who wanted to strengthen their resume, learn basic computer skills, and help them improve their interview skills. My job was to sit with these guests and ask how they were doing, what was going on in their lives, and see if there was any other way our organization could be of support. This time was very special because I could connect with guests on a one-on-one basis, hear their stories, and offer a prayer for them.

A gentleman I mentored was very serious about his success. He was coming to the program every day, walking an hour and a half from the park he was sleeping in to get to class on time. When we found this out, we gave him bus fare so that he didn't have to walk so far. When he was down to the last week of the program, he had an interview for a full-time job. He promised to come back and tell me how things went. About a week later he asked for a moment of my time and if I could step away from my desk. We sat down together, and he was trying to seem very serious, but I could tell he was holding back a smile. After a little beating around the bush, he finally told me that he landed the job. I jumped up, we hugged, and I congratulated him. It was his persistence and hard work that got him to a new stage in his life, and his willingness to seek the help offered to him. This man had the persistence of Hannah, refusing to let the obstacles in his life stop him from succeeding. For anyone who has a need or a struggle, know that you are a beloved child of God, and you are valuable and worth the persistence. For those in the church who are doing well and have enough to share, let us respond as Christ would to persistent people and share our blessings honoring their value. We can become advocates.

Eli shows us how not to be an advocate through his mistake of judging Hannah. Once Hannah defends herself, Eli realizes his error; he had been quick to judge her and make assumptions about her intentions and her character. He then shifts his focus to advocating with her, telling her to go in peace and that the God of Israel will grant her the petition she has made. This is Eli's Job as a priest, to use his platform to speak to God for others. So, he used his platform so that Hannah could be heard.

When I was in college I was exposed to outreach, missions, social justice, and evangelism through our chapel program. Speakers from the United States and from all over the world would come and tell us about their ministries. These included helping persecuted Christians, nonprofit organizations that sold fair trade gifts, and orphanages that helped connect families. As a girl who had grown up fairly sheltered from the world, I felt like my eyes had been opened to injustice and how Christians should be bringing messages of hope. My heart was stirred, and I wanted to take action and become an advocate. I was very passionate and fervent in my new understanding of the world, and I remember that I adopted the phrase, "being a voice for the voiceless." While this came from a good place with good intentions, I had my over-zealous bubble popped rather abruptly. One of my professors kindly, but firmly said that we don't advocate *for* people but *with* people. The professor also told me that there is no such thing as a voiceless person; instead, those of us who have a voice in society could choose to step back so that other voices can be heard. I learned that what I had was known as a "savior complex"; I thought that my actions would help me swoop in and save the day. I would gain satisfaction and gratification from helping and doing good in the world. But this wasn't the right way to advocate, because I was really making advocacy about myself: my desires to help and to be a helpful person would easily get in the way of the desires and needs of those who I intended to help. The priest Eli learned this lesson too. He misjudged the situation and *spoke on Hannah's behalf.* She corrected him with her needs and desires, and he changed his behavior. Eli then blesses Hannah with *her* needs as the priority, using his platform as a priest to step back and let her voice be heard.

I saw the best way to advocate also at the OAC. One gentleman I worked with had just gotten into some housing and was preparing for job interviews. He was very positive and upbeat about his future, and he was grateful for my help in getting his birth certificate. It was required for our paperwork that we ask why he was requesting a birth certificate. He told me he needed his documentation to access his veteran benefits. He was both amazed and frustrated with the veteran benefits available to him; he was amazed at how much his life was improving because he had access to benefits, but he was frustrated that there were so many veterans sleeping on the streets who didn't know what programs and opportunities were available to them. He told me that he was going to be just fine and not to worry about him. He decided to use his voice and new platform to help veterans' voices would find a place to be heard. This was an important lesson for me about advocacy, and I believe this man reflects the voice of Eli who advocated with Hannah. For those of us that have a voice in society, a platform from which we are heard, or any type of influence, large or small, let us use those opportunities to uplift the voices of others and listen closely to the desires and needs of the people who are persisting against obstacles in society.

After this encounter in the temple, Hannah soon conceives a son. Hannah is so thankful to God for the answer to her prayer that she names him Samuel because she had asked for him from the Lord. Hannah not only dedicates Samuel's namesake to God, but she dedicates *him* to the temple. When Samuel is old enough to be weaned, Hannah brings him to the temple to be committed to the Lord. She leaves him there to learn and live under Eli the priest. The is the ultimate act of gratitude: to give away the child that she so desperately desired to the service of the Lord. Hannah responded with gratitude by emptying herself, and God's blessings were multiplied through Samuel's life of being a prophet and judge. Author Ann Voskamp explains in her book *1000 Gifts* that living a life of gratitude means trusting that "there is always enough God." God has no end, and if we are blessed then in our gratitude, we bless others without fear that we will run out of God's blessings. Just like Hannah, Ann Voskamp says that we empty ourselves to fill others and be filled by the goodness of God.

That is the cycle of gratitude, we receive, we give thanks, and we give back. This is the cycle we see in Hannah's story: persistence, advocacy, and giving thanks.

Beloved, let us know our worth and persist in our desires and needs. God wants to fulfill our needs. We can be brave and tell our truth like Hannah. Let us be a part of fulfilling those needs by being advocates. When we are a blessed people, we need not fear scarcity but live in abundance. There is enough God for all, and we can participate in God's goodness. We can learn, like Eli, to advocate with people and amplify their voices. Then together let us give thanks and praise to God by engaging in joy and continuing to share and love one another. Samuel was a gift given to Hannah but she shared that gift with all of Israel. In our posture of gratitude, let us respond as faithful people, as the Body of Christ, to love and serve all.

Narrative Retelling of Job: Approaching Grace with Boldness
Job 23:1-9, 16-17

Job 23:1-9, 16-17
Then Job answered: "Today also my complaint is bitter; his hand is heavy despite my groaning.

Oh, that I knew where I might find him, that I might come even to his dwelling! I would lay my case before him, and fill my mouth with arguments. I would learn what he would answer me, and understand what he would say to me. Would he contend with me in the greatness of his power? No; but he would give heed to me. There an upright person could reason with him, and I should be acquitted forever by my judge. "If I go forward, he is not there; or backward, I cannot perceive him; on the left he hides, and I cannot behold him; I turn to the right, but I cannot see him. God has made my heart faint; the Almighty has terrified me; If only I could vanish in darkness, and thick darkness would cover my face!

Hebrews 4:12-16
Indeed, the word of God is living and active, sharper than any two-edged sword, piercing until it divides soul from spirit, joints from marrow; it is able to judge the thoughts and intentions of the heart. And before him no creature is hidden, but all are naked and laid bare to the eyes of the one to whom we must render an account. Since, then, we have a great high priest who has passed through the heavens, Jesus, the Son of God, let us hold fast to our confession. For we do not have a high priest who is unable to sympathize with our weaknesses, but we have one who in every respect has been tested as we are, yet without sin. Let us therefore approach the throne of grace with boldness, so that we may receive mercy and find grace to help in time of need.

When I read this Hebrews passage of God's word being a two-edged sword that cuts, slices, lays bare, so that someone can be examined, I could only think of the trials of Job. In the second part of the scripture, that talks about approaching the throne of grace with boldness, I could only think of Job who spoke boldly and honestly with a rawness that is shocking. Job is cut down by God's word, and his faith is examined. Job says harsh things to God and about God, and yet God shows up and shows Job grace. Not so coincidentally, Job was also one of the assigned Old Testament passages for this morning that was assigned by the lectionary. So, I will provide a narrative retelling of Job, weaving in the book of Hebrews into the story. May you hear a new word, gain fresh insight, and hear the good news of the Gospel from this well-known Bible story:

There once was a man from the land of Uz whose name was Job. He was blameless, upright, turned away from evil, and feared God. He had a wife, three daughters, seven sons, hundreds of sheep, oxen, and donkeys, thousands of camels, and many servants. Job was a faithful man who was very blessed, who rose early in the morning to give burnt offerings for all of his family...*just* in case they had sinned. While Job was relishing his rich life on earth, the heavenly beings gathered and presented themselves to the Lord. Questions arose about Job's character among the heavenly beings. Was Job really faithful? Or did he just appear faithful because he had been so blessed? Would he be so pious if he wasn't so blessed? Satan, the Accuser approached and asked God, "Does Job fear God for nothing? Have you not put a fence around him and his house and all that he has, on every side? You have blessed the work of his hands, and his possessions have increased in the land. But stretch out your hand now, and touch all that he has, and he will curse you to your face." God caught onto the rising suspicion and agreed to let Satan the Accuser have power over

Job's family and belongings, with one condition. God said, "Only do not stretch out your hand against him." The word of God was alive and active, spoken to judge the thoughts and intentions of Job's heart.

It happened in an instant. All in one day Job lost everything. He was blindsided when a few surviving servants came breathlessly running to tell him that Sabeans and Chaldeans came to raid his livestock and killed his servants, that a fire from heaven fell down to kill the rest of his livestock and servants, and that a great wind knocked down the house of the eldest son killing all of Job's children. In just a blink, everything and everyone that Job had or cared for was gone. In a rush of grief, Job stood and tore his clothes, then shaved his head and stripped bare, saying, "Naked I came from my mother's womb, and naked shall I return there; the Lord gave, and the Lord has taken away; blessed be the name of the Lord." The living word of God laid Job naked and bare so that he might render an account of his actions; and that he did. Job did not curse God; but the Accuser wasn't yet convinced. So, Satan went before God again, and again God consented to let the Accuser take control so long as Job's life was spared. Just when Job thought he had nothing left to lose, Satan inflicted loathsome sores on his entire body, from the sole of his feet to the crown of his head. Job, now a broken man, sat on the ground, slowly scraping his skin with a potsherd. The two-edge sword that is the word of God pierced Job, divided his soul from his spirit. He was mourning, miserable, and distressed.

Job's friends found him sitting on the ground in an unrecognizable state. Eliphaz the Temanite, Bildad the Shuhite, and Zophar the Naamathite came to sit with him on the ground with him for seven days. They sat together, in the pain and in the silence, for a week. Sitting in the pain with a friend is the most powerful thing a person can do. However, these three friends made the mistake that every person eventually makes: they got uncomfortable with the pain and began saying unhelpful things to try to "fix" it for Job. When people get uncomfortable with sitting in the pain they try to make sense of it, saying there must be a reason behind it, that maybe the person who is experiencing pain somehow brought upon themselves. Or even worse, there are the platitudes like, God will never give you more than you can handle, which anyone who has experienced loss or tragedy will say is untrue. Job was not handling it. This is the mistake we have all made at some point when our friends and family suffer, and this is what Job's friends did.

Eliphaz said, "Those who plow iniquity sow trouble and reap the same." Bildad told Job to make a "supplication to the Almighty." Zophar warned Job that, "God exacts of you less than your guilt deserves." Together they said that Job had created trouble, so he was reaping trouble; he must repent because he has gotten the punishment that his sins deserved. These words were spoken to try to fix what was happening, but they only served to kick Job while he was down. This cycle repeated itself 3 times where Eliphaz condemns Job, Job defends himself, Bildad condemns, Jobs defends, Zophar condemns, Job defends, and it starts all over again with Eliphaz. Over and over again these friends slammed Job with accusations and with shallow comfort. Surely Job must have done something to deserve all this right? These friends could only come to this conclusion. Any other conclusion might have threatened their understanding of God; it was easier for them to beat up on Job than it was for them to assess whether or not their beliefs and their theology might need to be challenged, questioned, and stretched. They chose to guard their beliefs instead of showing compassion to Job.

Job stood firm and bold. Each time one of his friends came after him, Job defended himself. Job called out to God, demanded answers and sought out help. Truly, this is what it means to approach the throne of grace with boldness when he said, "I loathe my life! I curse the day I was born. Oh, that it would please God to crush me. My complaint is bitter! God has made my heart faint; The Almighty has terrified me." Such strong and powerful words that Job dared to speak aloud to his friends and to God can be a shock to hear; and yet scripture said he never cursed or sinned when he spoke. Job said, "God has crushed me with a tempest; if it is a contest of strength, God is the strong one! How will you, my friends, comfort me? Your answers are nothing but falsehoods." These are the words of a man who had nothing and no one, who was only left to defend himself with boldness. If his friends could not answer him, who was left?

There was one more friend who has been silent this entire time, a young man named Elihu. One would think a fresh set of eyes and a new perspective would be a breath of fresh air for this toxic cycle of despair. But Elihu rebuked Job as well, and said, "You said I am clean without transgression, but you are not right. Why do you contend against God?" It would be easy to dismiss Elihu, but he provided a segue into what was to be the living, active, and physically present word of God. Elihu told Job about the elusive wisdom and action of God, and said, "God is greater than any mortal. For God speaks in one way, and in two, though people do not perceive it. See, God is exalted in power. Who is a teacher like God?" Elihu explained that Job and all people do not see what God is at work doing in all of God's wisdom. There had to be something happening behind the scenes that no one was aware of.

This is when the word of God became living and active in a completely new way when God directly answered Job. God made a theatrical entrance by way of whirlwind. From this whirlwind God declared, "Who is this that darkens counsel by words without knowledge? Where were you when I laid the foundation of the earth? Have you commanded the morning since your days began, and caused the dawn to know its place, so that it might take hold of the skirts of the earth, and the wicked be shaken out of it? Look at Behemoth, which I made just as I made you; it eats grass like an ox. Its bones are tubes of bronze, its limbs like bars of iron. Can you draw out Leviathan with a fishhook, or press down its tongue with a cord? Its breath kindles coals, and a flame comes out of its mouth." God told of the wonders of creation with incredible and mighty animals like behemoth and leviathan. God spoke of the wisdom of the cosmos, that no one else has but God. How can someone like Job judge God when Job doesn't have the wisdom of all creation? Job repented in dust and ashes.

Here comes the twist, and the surprise of this distressing story: God said that the friends had not spoken what is right about God, but Job had. The friends had defended God, or at least their beliefs about God; Job was the one who defended himself and said shocking, audacious things about God. Job had dared to approach the throne of grace with boldness, and God approved of the rawness and honesty that Job brought before the throne. God's wrath was kindled against the friends who had to go and sacrifice burnt offerings. God's compassion is shown when Job's possessions and family are restored. There is no pretty bow to tie up this story neatly with a satisfying resolution, because Job still suffered, and his previous family was gone forever. Maybe that is the point: life is messy, God's word is often unclear, but God always shows up in the mess.

So, let us learn from Job that when we cannot grasp divine wisdom and when God's word cuts us like a two-edged sword, we are allowed to approach the throne of grace boldly, honestly, daringly, baring our souls and seeking compassion.

Who May Dwell on Your Holy Hill?
Psalm 15

O LORD, who may abide in your tent?
   Who may dwell on your holy hill?

Those who walk blamelessly, and do what is right,
   and speak the truth from their heart;
who do not slander with their tongue,
   and do no evil to their friends,
   nor take up a reproach against their neighbors;

in whose eyes the wicked are despised,
   but who honor those who fear the LORD;
who stand by their oath even to their hurt;
who do not lend money at interest,
   and do not take a bribe against the innocent.

Those who do these things shall never be moved.

Often when we think of where God is, it has been a long-standing tradition to believe that God is up in the sky high above, looking down on creation and that by going to church we can enter into a sacred place where we can access God. Here we see the Psalmist poetically and artistically describe the presence of God who abides in the tent and dwells on the holy hill. Again, we see a mixing of the images of sacred spaces to access God and the elevated place where God is perceived to be. The Psalmist asks, who may live in these places with God? In the Hebrew scriptures we learn that the tabernacle or the tent was where the Ark of the Covenant was kept, and that the Ark was believed to be the physical presence of God with the

Israelites. The "holy hill" is an artistic way of expressing the dwelling place of God, in a high place looking down, and it is seen in numerous other psalms.

It is tempting to only hear the first part of this psalm and believe the notion that we have to go to a specific place to find God, to be with God. While we create these sacred places like our churches to worship God, to find peace, and to learn about our faith, we do not abide here. We do not dwell here. And maybe that's the point: we aren't supposed to. We abide in homes with families, with neighbors next door, hospitals down the road, grocery stores a few blocks away, school buildings full of people, pharmacies, libraries, businesses, and soup kitchens all surrounding our dwelling places. This is good news, because scripture tells us over and over again that God is not limited to one place; God was in the wilderness with the Hebrews when they were liberated from Egypt, God met prophets like Moses and Elijah on mountain tops, the prophet Ezekiel saw a vision of the glory of God leaving the temple to go be with the Jews in exile, Jesus came as the incarnation of God to be with us, and Christ will return again to bring heaven to earth. The God of our church, the God of the tent and the tabernacle, is also God with us. God is with us facing the stress at work, the conflict with our families, the various health battles, the homeless on the streets, and the injustices in our institutions. Although we find peace here in our church buildings, we cannot hide from the problems of the world in our churches, clinging to a safe sanctuary, assuming that this is the only place to find God. God is out amongst our neighbors; to embrace our neighbors is to embrace God.

We already abide in God's kingdom, but the new heaven and new earth is still yet to come. This is when we truly will understand what it means to dwell with God. In his book *Secrets in the Dark* Reverend Frederick Buechner describes a time when he was driving into New York City, and the everyday streets revealed to him what the kingdom of God might look like. He looked around the city on an average day when nothing in particular was different from what he had seen before, but somehow everything was different from his fresh perspective on this new day. He saw the streets alive with traffic and shoppers, people of all races living and moving together in one place. After parking the car, he saw people eating their lunches outdoors, some dressed in business suits that cost hundreds of dollars, others dressed in sneakers and jeans. They were peacefully eating their sandwiches together in silence, young and old next to each other flooded in light, surrounded by green foliage. Buechner watched a clown in the park blow up a balloon, "sneakily" twisting it into what he described as a "dove of peace" and handed it to an awe-struck boy. He then describes a middle-aged woman who walked past him on the sidewalk and said very quietly without even breaking her pace, "Jesus loves you." He was taken aback by such a declaration in this place that he was seeing as if for the first time. Buechner elucidates that in this moment as he was walking the streets, he felt as if they were streets of gold and this is what the kingdom of God might be. He explains that we can live into the kingdom around us, with hope for the kingdom to come if we turn away from madness, cruelty, and blindness, and turn toward tolerance, hope, sanity and justice.

Each week we gather here for a worship service, but once we leave the building, we are called to continue worshiping God. In the second part of the psalm there are instructions on the conduct we are to live by: we are to be those who walk blamelessly, and do what is right, speak the truth, do not slander, and do no evil to their friends, nor take up a reproach against their neighbors; who fear the Lord, who stand by their oath, who do not lend money with interest, and do not take a bribe against the innocent. There is a community in Georgia, which I believe lives these standards well. This faith community known as "Koinonia" which is the Greek word for a particular type of fellowship with Christians and God. The Koinonia group was established by Clarence Jordan in 1942. It is an intentional community that was created to reflect the kingdom of God on earth, where people are invited to live together as group to share their lives as extended family. They refused to participate in racial segregation prior to the civil rights era, they pool their financial resources to support one another, and they worship God together. They are not closed off from the world; instead they hope that this community will be a demonstration of God's kingdom, knowing that their path to following God is specific and unique. They hope to inspire other communities to follow their own unique path in honoring God, so that the spiritual fruit that people bear will be obvious both to members of the church and nonmembers. Living in this type of community in the modern world doesn't work for most of us, but it can serve as inspiration to walk blamelessly by standing up against injustice, to honor and fear God by seeking out more people who we can be spiritual family with, and not lending money with interest by sharing our financial resources as we are able to do with no strings attached.

In the third part of the Psalm it says that "those who do these things shall never be moved." Since this Psalm focuses on living with God, this part of the scripture can be interpreted to say that we cannot be moved, removed, or shaken from the presence of God. Those who do these things will never be moved from living with God; that doesn't mean we are to be still and motionless. Our faith moves us to pray, to speak to God, which we should do. Thoughts and prayers can be offered in our homes and in our places of worship as our compassion inspires our hearts to intercede on behalf of others. But our words must also be paired with action. Rabbi Abraham Joshua Heschel was a Jewish scholar who was deported from Germany in the Nazi regime in 1938. He became an activist, moved to American in 1940, and marched with Martin Luther King Jr. in Selma, Alabama to Montgomery in 1965. When he reflected on this march, he said that he felt like his legs were praying. When this Rabbi was deported, he was not moved from God. When he moved to America he was not moved from God. When he marched for Civil Rights he was not moved from God. And yet Rabbi Heschel never stopped moving. Everyone has different physical abilities and different skills they can use to put their prayers into action. Whether this means picking up a phone and making an important call to leaders to demand action, going out to volunteer time to charities, becoming a community leader and organizer, getting involved in the outreach with our church, writing letters to advocate for others, or donating money to causes that show Christ's love in the world, we can use what we have with what we are able to do by praying with our hands and feet paired with our spoken prayers to God. Since we cannot be moved from the presence of God, God goes with us as we enact our prayers.

God lives in holy and sacred spaces, and all places are made holy by God's presence. Our dwelling place is not on some far-off holy hill, removed from the world. We abide here in God's world where God is here with us. The kingdom of God is already among us; perhaps it looks like an average day in New York City, or a community on Georgia, or like protesters praying with their legs. We've been tasked with living blamelessly, being kind to our friends and neighbors, and being generous with our resources as we wait for kingdom come. We cannot accomplish this by standing still; we move, knowing that we will never be moved from God's presence. Let us take heart in God's presence that dwells where we dwell.

Longing for God
Psalm 42

As a deer longs for flowing streams,
 so my soul longs for you, O God.
My soul thirsts for God,
 for the living God.
When shall I come and behold
 the face of God?
My tears have been my food
 day and night,
while people say to me continually,
 "Where is your God?"

These things I remember,
 as I pour out my soul:
how I went with the throng,
 and led them in procession to the house of God,
with glad shouts and songs of thanksgiving,
 a multitude keeping festival.
Why are you cast down, O my soul,
 and why are you disquieted within me?
Hope in God; for I shall again praise him,
 my help and my God.

My soul is cast down within me;
 therefore I remember you
from the land of Jordan and of Hermon,
 from Mount Mizar.
Deep calls to deep
 at the thunder of your cataracts;
all your waves and your billows
 have gone over me.

> By day the LORD commands his steadfast love,
>   and at night his song is with me,
>   a prayer to the God of my life.
>
> I say to God, my rock,
>   "Why have you forgotten me?
> Why must I walk about mournfully
>   because the enemy oppresses me?"
> As with a deadly wound in my body,
>   my adversaries taunt me,
> while they say to me continually,
>   "Where is your God?"
>
> Why are you cast down, O my soul,
>   and why are you disquieted within me?
> Hope in God; for I shall again praise him,
>   my help and my God.

Recently, my husband and I took a trip to New Orleans. We knew that we had to enjoy some jazz while we were in town, so we bought tickets to listen to the All Stars, a Dixieland band complete with trombone, trumpet, clarinet, drums, saxophone, piano, and doghouse bass. We were part of the first group of people inside this small, one room building. We all packed in tight, shoulder to shoulder, with complete strangers so that we could make room to squeeze in as many people as possible. In these close quarters we were already toasty and sweaty, but the suffocating Louisiana humidity only added to the heat. However, once the musicians entered, the energy changed and the dancing, clapping, cheering, and singing began. The heat and lack of personal space was quickly forgotten as we were swept away by the upbeat music that was full of joy and celebration. Suddenly, I realized I was worshipping! In that moment God had showed up in that Dixieland jazz. We were singing together with hospitality and joy as if we were all intimate friends. I could have stayed there the rest of night listening and dancing. The music was holy to me because I knew that the raucous joy in the music was a form of resilience and defiance. Jazz was born in a time of oppression by the very people who were oppressed. It was a way to create and celebrate life in the face of those who tried to hold them back through laws of segregation. I knew that jazz was an important part of African American history, and God was present in the creation of this music. I also realized that this history linked all the way back to the spirituals that slaves would sing. These spirituals were sung to God as an act of defiance to slave owners, calling to God for liberation. These songs were prayers, with and without words in the lyrics of the spirituals and in the blare of the jazz trumpet. These prayers didn't ask questions or demand answers but asked for God to be present and liberate those who were crying out. God's presence, God's deliverance, and the music helped people battle oppression.

Here we also see that the Psalmist is crying out as his soul longs for and thirsts for the living God. His hope is in God, even when his soul is disquieted within him. When it is dark in the night, God's song is with him. Just as the deer pants for water, the Psalmist longs for God and is overcome by God's waves and billows as deep calls out to deep. While oppression is a reality, the Psalmist finds resilience through the poetry of the Psalm, calling out to God to encompass him in God's presence. He asks God, "Why have you forgotten me? Why must I walk about mournfully because the enemy oppresses me?" However, there is no response to these questions, and the Psalmist can still find peace in hoping in God. God is with him, even as he struggles and is oppressed, walking on this journey with him.

Often when we face hardship, we immediately look for a reason or an answer, crying out to God and asking why like the Psalmist. Sometimes we even look for someone to blame, picking out entire religions or ethnicities to point our fingers at. We know deep in our hearts that blame, and even answers, doesn't bring satisfaction, because when tragedy strikes all that we really wish for is the atrocity to be undone. When we don't have answers, sometimes we lean on platitudes such as, "There's a reason for everything." While this may comfort some and is offered to those grieving with compassion and good intentions, there are many people who, in the throes of tragedy, do not want to hear those phrases. Often despair and pain do not make any sense; there isn't a rhyme or reason in the chaos. When people ask us why these things happen, instead of offering platitudes, we don't have to be afraid to say, "I don't know." In fact, saying "I don't know" can be a mighty act of faith, relying on God's grace to be ever present and fill in the cracks of our limited knowledge. We may not know why, but what we do know is that God is our rock and our help.

When our souls are cast down and disquieted within us, we desperately desire to behold the face of God. When people turn to the church to find God, we must be ready to show that God is present with us. As the church it can be challenging to faithfully respond to tragic events when we don't have all the answers that people are looking for. In her book *Accidental Saints* author Nadia-Bolz Weber tells a story of how her church practiced being present in tragedy in order to show the community God's presence representing a God who weeps and suffers with us. She and the church that she pastors held a Good Friday service where they read the liturgy for the service and sang the hymn "Were You There When They Crucified My Lord?" Then the church members drove over to a local neighborhood to continue their worship. They stood in the dark with no street lights or sidewalks and loud guard dogs barking nearby as they gathered around an empty home which had been the scene of a grisly crime. In this home a mother named Mayra Perez shot her three children and herself just a month prior, with only one child surviving the incident. The congregation laid purple tulips and a crucifix made of tree branches in the yard. Then they sang to God, changing the words of the hymn saying, "Were you there when Mayra Perez took three lives?" After singing they entered a time of silent prayer. As they prayed even the dogs who had been barking fell silent. A week later, one of Nadia's friends called and said that one of the families noticed a group of random Christians gathered around the house where the murder/suicide took place. The family saw them singing and praying, and the people of the community were grateful that this church had brought a sense of healing. In the dark of that night, Nadia and the congregation had no idea anyone was watching. This group of people knew that the community was panting like a deer for God's healing waters, and so they brought their songs, prayers, and presence. They acknowledged the tragedy and helped the people of the neighborhood whose souls thirsted find the presence of the living God.

While the Psalmist's soul is cast down, he remembers. He remembers God was present in the land of Jordan and the land of Hermon from Mount Mizar. We go out into our communities and address the needs so that they can remember God, too. A week ago, our country was devasted by the shooting at the Pulse night club in Orlando, Florida. 49 people were killed, and this loss has been felt not only in Florida, but in all of our hearts. Over this past week we have seen how people have responded by showing up in long lines to give 28,000 pints of blood to help save the survivors of the shooting. I do not know if everyone who showed up to give blood are people of faith, but there is no doubt in my mind that this is the Holy Spirit at work, showing up to embrace the wounded and the grieving. We as the church can learn from the witness of those who showed up to donate blood to the survivors of the Pulse shooting. When tragedy strikes, we give blood, donate money, buy groceries, and hold vigils so that our communities can see an active church, a living God.

We must also be prepared to meet the people where they are in their struggle when they walk through our church doors. While we may be tempted to try and offer our own answers and platitudes, we can offer our hospitality instead. Hospitality in our churches should be reminiscent of the hospitality we show in our homes. When I was a young girl it was always a treat to go spend the weekend at my grandparents' house. They always stocked the house with treats and had a warm grilled cheese waiting for my sister and me. They would take us on trips, read us stories, and prepare hot bubble baths with lots of toys. They made their home our home so that we felt welcomed, special, and loved. If we consider our church buildings a home where all are welcome, then when people step through the doors, we must be ready. When we see someone new, let's say, "Welcome! Would you like to sit with me? I've got a space just for you." Or when people come with pain and grief, we must be ready to offer a tissue, hold their hand, and cry with them. When people can't pray, let us pray for them. When they can't sing, let us sing loud enough for them and us. When others can't believe, let us believe enough on their behalf. This is how we show the presence of God to them, and how we also experience the love of God. When we support each other while being present in their struggles, the steadfast love from the Lord will be seen in the day and will follow us as a song in the night, when all seems dark and when we need it the most.

When we are at a loss for words, answers, or understanding, our souls are thirsting for the living God. We remember that God is our help, our hope, and our rock when we find resilience in music that overcomes oppression. When the deep of pain calls out to the deep of compassion, God's thundering cataracts and waves billow over mourning communities when we acknowledge tragedy and are present in the community. When people wander into our sanctuaries, panting like deer for water, we help them behold the face of God by welcoming them in. We may not have all the answers when people ask us, "Where is your God?" But we can let them know that God is present with us, weeping with our pain with arms open for comfort. And maybe that's all the answer we need. By day the Lord commands steadfast love, God's song is with us in the night, and this is our prayer for our lives.

The Light We've Been Given
Psalm 50:1-6

The mighty one, God the Lord,
  speaks and summons the earth
  from the rising of the sun to its setting.
Out of Zion, the perfection of beauty,
  God shines forth.

Our God comes and does not keep silence,
  before him is a devouring fire,
  and a mighty tempest all around him.
He calls to the heavens above
  and to the earth, that he may judge his people:
"Gather to me my faithful ones,
  who made a covenant with me by sacrifice!"
The heavens declare his righteousness,
  for God himself is judge.

In her book *When God is Silent* author Barbara Brown Taylor says that, "Many people pray for an encounter with the living God. Those whose prayers are answered rarely ask for the same thing twice." She says that this is because, "We are not up to direct encounter with God. We want it but we don't want it. Safe fire is our own invention." This Psalm is about that very experience, an encounter with God that is described by King David's chief musician Asaph as a devouring fire. The fire is before God, who is surrounded by a mighty tempest while summoning the earth and calling to the heavens. This vivid imagery describes God shining forth and recalling the covenant made with the faithful. Such a powerful and direct communication from God shines a light that perfectly illuminates God's love and truth. While we are focusing on the Psalm this morning, we remember that today is Transfiguration Sunday. We recall when Jesus took Peter, James, and John up on a mountain and became transfigured, clothed in white and surrounded by light. God claimed Jesus as his son, confirming Jesus' authority. This revelation was an irrefutable affirmation of Jesus' power and mission, and only Peter, James, and John were able to witness this event.

Often, we crave such a crystal-clear revelation from God, praying for a message of understanding and guidance in times of doubt. We seek an undeniable light that cuts through all darkness. These major revelations transform us in an instant; they transform our doubts into certainty and our fears into courage. But God's revelation comes in God's timing, and usually to a very specific audience. We are not in control of when God speaks, what God says, or how God delivers the message. As Barbara Brown Taylor says, God is not a safe fire, but a consuming one. In this Psalm, God is not just coming to gather the faithful, but to judge the people. God's light opens our eyes to the beauty of righteousness, but also to the transformation that must occur within us so that we might live a righteous life. This phenomenon of incredible magnitude can only be initiated by an all-powerful Creator, and this is not going to be an everyday occurrence. We would get complacent with daily transfigurations, and they would lose their impact. But that doesn't mean we aren't given sources of light and left to stumble in the darkness. If we pay attention and keep our eyes open, we may see small graces shining around us. It may not be the earth-shaking experience that we want, or may think that we want, but how we respond to these sources of light can truly be transformative over time. God is patient and works in our hearts slowly and lovingly, transforming us into righteous people. The smaller lights in our lives that we might overlook can be the catalyst we need for our souls to be transformed.

Wonder, joy, praise, and gratitude are all aspects that can grow our spiritual lives for transformation. Seeing God's grace in the glory that is creation is a beacon of light that is shining for all to see. It takes time to stop and look at the beauty of creation that is right beneath our noses, but it is a worthwhile endeavor.

In *1000 Gifts* author Ann Voskamp writes about her life as a farmer's wife and being a mother of seven. She practices gratitude by seeing God's grace in everyday life. She does this by taking time out of her busy schedule to pause, to notice, to look around, and to wonder. One of these moments comes just as she is finishing preparing dinner one night. Ann's husband comes in from finishing his duties on the farm as her hungry kids wait anxiously for dinner, and he tells her that she must see what's outside. She's reluctant to go, knowing that she's about to serve dinner, but decides to take this moment to practice gratitude. She walks outside to her porch to see an enormous, bright harvest moon. It seems so close that she can almost touch it. In fact, she decides to try. Ann takes off in a sprint across the wheat field outside her home, running as if she was four years old again and chasing fireflies. She reaches the edge of the field where she is as close to the moon as she can be. She takes time to stop and marvel, and then she falls to her knees in praise of God's glory. Her kids came chasing after their mother who has clearly been enraptured by the joy of God's light, and they all giggle in wonder together, completely forgetting about dinner. Often what we are searching for when we ask for God's mighty revelation, is really intimacy with God. Taking time to pause and notice the beauty and light already around us in God's world is a great place to begin to find that intimacy. Intimacy invites God's transformation into our lives.

There are times when the craving for intimacy deepens into a more persistent, ongoing problem of loneliness. A dear friend of mine took me to Vogel State Park in North Georgia to do some hiking and to see some waterfalls. This was a special place for her, and she visited this area often. She told me that once she was driving alone in a small town nearby the park early one morning. It was still dark and very foggy. She had been driving for a while, and the quiet and darkness began to make her feel lonely. It's easy to feel all alone in the world when someone goes long stretches of time without any human interaction. As she continued down the road she noticed a tiny light in the distance. As she drove closer, she realized that the light was coming from the porch of a small Baptist church sitting on top of a hill. The light wasn't especially bright, but it stood out in the darkness and fog around her. It was a sign of life within the community. It made her feel less alone, brightened her spirits, and encouraged her on her journey. When someone feels as if they are no longer alone and that the weight of their burden is being shared with others, then deep-seated issues can be faced with courage. Perhaps someone with depression, anxiety, or PTSD sees God's light shining in the soft glow of the lamp in the therapist's office. Maybe someone suffering from addiction sees God's light in the fluorescent bulbs that illuminate the circle of chairs of their recovery group where stories and secrets are held in safety. Someone grieving a recent loss may possibly glimpse the flickering light of God in the candles held by the mourning community at the vigil. Responding to these sparks of light in times of despairing loneliness can make a path for healing. When we heal, we are transformed.

Light can move us toward a more just world that ends oppression. We remember this especially now during Black History Month when we think about how far we've come with racial reconciliation and how far we have left to go. When we remember the Underground Railroad, which is the system of pathways and homes slaves used to escape from their masters to obtain freedom, we know that they travelled in the darkness of night. A popular spot to cross over into freedom was over the Ohio River from Kentucky into Ohio. John Rankin was a stationmaster on the Underground Railroad, which meant that his home was open to slaves escaping to freedom. He would use a lantern at night to signal when it was safe to cross the Ohio River and find shelter in his home. It was a beacon of hope and freedom to those who were seeking liberation but was small enough not to gain too much attention from hostile eyes. We also think of the song "Follow the Drinking Gourd" which has often been associated with secret codes for escape routes on the Underground Railroad. It is believed that the drinking gourd refers to the star constellation known as the "Big Dipper," and some believe that this song uses the Big Dipper and other pathways as a method for escaping to freedom. This has not been historically confirmed, and many believe that this song comes from folklore. Regardless of whether this spiritual reflects a historical narrative or comes from legends and traditions, the guiding light of the stars stands as a symbol of hope for freedom and justice. These minor lights of lanterns and stars had major impacts. A light, even a small light, can pierce the darkness in a way that empowers others in pursuit of a more just world, if only we respond to that light. Justice and righteousness transform the world.

The transfiguration is a divine mystery. What happened to Jesus on the mountain baffles us. Why it happened, how it happened, what it means, and why it was only revealed to a few people can be absolutely confounding. In our Psalm we see that God comes forth to shine, initiating an interaction with the covenantal people to gather and to judge. Any revelation is a powerful gift from God, but this means we receive God in full force, encompassed by the devouring fire and mighty tempest. We crave the clarifying, undeniable truth that is illuminated by God's light, but this only comes from God and does not appear upon our command. Something so rare, so precious, and so terrifying cannot be contained and cannot be our only source of revitalization of faith. Instead, if we open our eyes to the light around us, we can respond faithfully and participate in being transformed into a righteous people. Pausing to allow the harvest moon to catch our eye for a few moments can lead to a time of praise. Seeking light in the community from the church on hill or in the office of a therapist can heal the damage of loneliness and share the burdens we carry with others who journey with us. Using the light that we have to point toward a more just world can guide others to freedom, like a lantern signaling safe passage in the night. Transfiguration offers an instant transformative experience, but we cannot summon that from our own whims. Instead, we are empowered to respond to the light we're given, no matter how small; the light we see peeking through the darkness on a daily basis, is how we are transformed over a lifetime. In this we can trust that God will gather us in as the faithful, constantly surrounded by God's light.

Labor for What Satisfies
Isaiah 55:1-9

Ho, everyone who thirsts, come to the waters; and you that have no money, come, buy and eat! Come, buy wine and milk without money and without price. Why do you spend your money for that which is not bread, and your labor for that which does not satisfy? Listen carefully to me, and eat what is good, and delight yourselves in rich food. Incline your ear, and come to me; listen, so that you may live. I will make with you an everlasting covenant, my steadfast, sure love for David. See, I made him a witness to the peoples, a leader and commander for the peoples. See, you shall call nations that you do not know, and nations that do not know you shall run to you, because of the LORD *your God, the Holy One of Israel, for he has glorified you. Seek the* LORD *while he may be found, call upon him while he is near; let the wicked forsake their way, and the unrighteous their thoughts; let them return to the* LORD, *that he may have mercy on them, and to our God, for he will abundantly pardon. For my thoughts are not your thoughts, nor are your ways my ways, says the* LORD. *For as the heavens are higher than the earth, so are my ways higher than your ways and my thoughts than your thoughts.*

An organization called Great Big Story shares narratives about beauty around the world and the human condition. One of these stories they tell is about the honey hunters of the Himalayas. The Bujon villagers in Nepal have an ancestral tradition of eating honey for strength and going hunting for a supply of it twice a year. A team takes their handmade rope ladders out into the jungle and climb up the side of a cliff where honeycombs hang. They risk numerous bee stings and falling hundreds of feet to their deaths for the sake of gathering precious honeycomb. They smoke out the bees with fires from below, killing as few as the can, and cut down the beehives. Then they hand-squeeze the honeycomb to extract the honey, bottle it up, and carry it out of the jungle back to their village. This honey not only nurtures their bodies, but this biannual event has been a tradition of their people for centuries. Honoring their ancestral traditions nourishes their souls. The honey hunters of the Himalayas labor for what satisfies them.

In the season of Lent when we are sacrificing, fasting, and abstaining like Jesus in the wilderness, it might sound odd to have a scripture text that speaks of feasting, indulging, and satisfaction. However, Isaiah addressed a parched and hungry people who had been exiled for so long. The Israelites had spent their Lenten season suffering and waiting for God's restoration. At long last there was some good news: God's abundant mercy and gracious provision were near! The bread, the wine, the milk, and the water were all free for the taking, no price set, no money necessary. In fact, it was their money and labor that had been spent on things which did not satisfy, not like this feast that God had prepared. Their labor had led them to stray from God's will. God was calling them to repent and enter into righteousness, so that they would readily receive pardon. God was redeeming the covenant made with David and was asking them to trust God's ways and thoughts over their own. Repentance was the labor they were being called to that would lead them to turn back to God's steadfast love. This did not mean that the Israelites had to work to earn God's love; on the contrary, the love was already being shown, and the table was already set. Repentance meant that the Israelites were willing to clear out sin to make room in their lives for goodness and grace. This was a sign that they had prepared their hearts for God's blessings and were willing to receive God's gracious gifts. Like the honey hunters of the Himalayas, they were being called to enter into this labor to satisfy their hunger, their thirst, and their spirits. It was a wholistic renewal. God's love would give them all that they needed for nourishment and survival; to repent was to labor for what satisfies. In Lent, we share in this season of laboring for repentance.

It's difficult to train a person's thinking from survival mode to abundant life. When someone has lived their entire life by fighting to survive, just barely scraping by, and estranged from any semblance of security or comfort, then unlearning being constantly in fight or flight mode can be an enormous undertaking. The Israelites had strived to survive as a people, and now God was calling them to thrive. God commanded them to listen so that they might live. God reminded them of the provision in the past through the covenant made with David; then God made a promise of provision for the future saying that their nation would be glorified and would inspire other nations to run to God, the Holy One of Israel. With God's promise before them, this could help the Israelites transition from their survival tactics to living an abundant life in God. To labor for what satisfies would help the Israelites to thrive. Sometimes we as the church find ourselves fighting our survival tactics. When we see that our congregations aren't growing as we'd hoped and some churches are even closing their doors for good, our fight or flight mindset can easily take control. However, if we take a moment to recognize and empower the skilled, talented people already in our pews and address the innumerable needs that exist within our own community, we can see that the Holy Spirit has fully equipped us to be a thriving witness of the Gospel of Jesus Christ that reveals God's love in the world.

Steven Hartman with CBS reports on an artist in Detroit named Richard Phillips who has an exhibit of his paintings, where each of his masterpieces sell for thousands of dollars. Richard is 73 years old and is just now receiving notoriety for his artistic talents; this is because he had been incarcerated for 46 years. In 1971 Richard was arrested for a murder that he didn't commit. While in prison, knowing he was innocent and that justice was not being served, he used his free time and energy to start painting. This was a constructive way to use the time he was unjustly serving to occupy his mind, his hands, and his skill. He used art as a survival tactic and created beauty from his scarcity. He was found innocent and freed In March of 2018; he had spent more time in prison than any other person who has ever been exonerated. As if this grave injustice committed against him wasn't enough, he *still* has not received the money that the state owes him for being wrongfully convicted. Richard was afraid that there would be no way for him to make a living, because he knew that no employer would hire him with his record and lack of job experience. Then he remembered all of his paintings that he had saved from his decades in prison. So he decided to sell his art. It hurts him to sell these treasured paintings that kept him focused and sustained during his imprisonment, but his years of hard work has helped him to survive and support himself after almost half a century of his life spent locked away. He transitioned into a more abundant living. Like the Israelites were being called to do, Richard had labored for what satisfied him, nourished his soul, and supported his livelihood so that he could survive and thrive.

Now we look inward and consider the labor that turns us to God's steadfast love. This Lenten season when we delve into our spiritual practices and disciplines within our faith walk, we can learn from the Israelites that this labor of repentance leads us to what satisfies us. God provides nourishment that renews and restores our whole selves, both in flesh and in spirit. Like the honey hunters of the Himalayas who labor for death-defying honeycombs and like Richard Phillips who labored to create art that helped him to survive and thrive, let us meditate on what we need to satisfy our souls. If we take time to remember God's faithfulness in the past and choose to trust in God's promises for the future, we can abandon our survival tactics and thrive in God's love. Like the Israelites, let us listen to God so that we may live. Let us pray about and then *act on* what God might be calling us to do. Speaking to a new friend, saying yes to a new job opportunity, volunteering at the homeless shelter, fostering a child, taking meals to a neighbor can all be nurturing for body and soul. God told the Israelites that their restoration would have the nations running toward them because of God's glory. That means that this invitation to God's feast of rich food extends out beyond Israel to *all* who forsake their wickedness; those who wish to partake must prepare their hearts and minds for God's provision. Should we answer this invitation we must labor in repentance to receive these promises, but it doesn't mean we have to work to earn them. The table is set with what satisfies us, all we have to do is show up.

Perceived Complexity
Isaiah 58:1-12

Shout out, do not hold back! Lift up your voice like a trumpet! Announce to my people their rebellion, to the house of Jacob their sins. Yet day after day they seek me and delight to know my ways, as if they were a nation that practiced righteousness and did not forsake the ordinance of their God; they ask of me righteous judgments, they delight to draw near to God. "Why do we fast, but you do not see? Why humble ourselves, but you do not notice?" Look, you serve your own interest on your fast day, and oppress all your workers. Look, you fast only to quarrel and to fight and to strike with a wicked fist. Such fasting as you do today will not make your voice heard on high. Is such the fast that I choose, a day to humble oneself? Is it to bow down the head like a bulrush, and to lie in sackcloth and ashes? Will you call this a fast, a day acceptable to the LORD? Is not this the fast that I choose: to loose the bonds of injustice, to undo the thongs of the yoke, to let the oppressed go free, and to break every yoke? Is it not to share your bread with the hungry, and bring the homeless poor into your house; when you see the naked, to cover them, and not to hide yourself from your own kin? Then your light shall break forth like the dawn, and your healing shall spring up quickly; your vindicator shall go before you, the glory of the LORD shall be your rear guard. Then you shall call, and the LORD will answer; you shall cry for help, and he will say, Here I am. If you remove the yoke from among you, the pointing of the finger, the speaking of evil, if you offer your food to the hungry and satisfy the needs of the afflicted, then your light shall rise in the darkness and your gloom be like the noonday. The LORD will guide you continually, and satisfy your needs in parched places, and make your bones strong; and you shall be like a watered garden, like a spring of water, whose waters never fail. Your ancient ruins shall be rebuilt; you shall raise up the foundations of many generations; you shall be called the repairer of the breach, the restorer of streets to live in.

In January of 2017 I was preparing for a two-week study abroad session in South Korea as part of my studies at Columbia Theological Seminary. I was greatly anticipating the trip, but I had no idea how the Holy Spirit was going to move. I was accompanied by two fantastic, brilliant professors and a group of my fellow classmates who quickly became my family. Of course, we were able to take in many sights, a vast amount of history, and delicious Korean food such as bulgogi and bibimbap; but most importantly we engaged with our siblings in Christ by learning about Christianity in South Korea and attending numerous worship services. The beautiful thing about traveling and engaging in another culture is that there are new opportunities to see different points of view that are insightful and challenging. One of the first lectures we heard as a group was delivered by a professor at Presbyterian University and Theological Seminary. This was the school that was hosting us during our stay. He was talking about how it is so easy to be caught up in the complexity of our daily lives that we become ignorant to the struggles of people within our country and the struggles that other countries endure. And then he challenged us with this question: are the lives of middle-class citizens in first world countries really that complex? We are busy people, but are we actually accomplishing anything in all of that busyness, or does it only serve as a distraction? This question challenged me, making me realize that we in America have the power, influence, and resources to affect the political, economic, and social aspects in our own country and in many other countries. And then I thought even further: if our church realized how much power is potentially at our finger tips, then how could we use it heal our nation and our relationships with the world?

In this passage we see that Isaiah is speaking to the people of Judah, proclaiming God's words of what true worship looks like. Isaiah says that the people of Judah "delight to draw near to God", but when they commit themselves to religious rituals such as fasting Isaiah says, "Look, you serve your own interest on your fast day, and oppress all your workers. Look, you fast only to quarrel and to fight and to strike with a wicked fist. Such fasting as you do today will not make your voice heard on high." Isaiah's prophetic words deliver God's message of conviction to the people of Judah, speaking to them as a group and a nation, as they are all guilty of this corporate sin. Here we see that God values a nation that "practiced righteousness" rather than seeks it through fasting. The Lord declares what is acceptable saying, "Is not this the fast I choose: to loose the bonds of injustice, to undo the thongs of the yoke, to let the oppressed go free and to break every yoke?" The words of the Lord continue to say that the people of Judah should share their bread with the hungry, their homes with the poor, and their clothes with the naked. The people of Judah have experienced exile, and now have returned to Judah. So, their lives are fairly complex. But are their lives so complex, so busy, that they should be distracted from the groans within their own community?

God is not discounting the corporate and private worship of the people of Judah. However, true worship includes seeing past one's own self-interest in appeasing God and goes further to break the yoke of oppression and loose the bonds of injustice. In Isaiah's prophecy, where there is conviction there is also good news. If the people follow God's commands to stop pointing fingers and speaking evil, and to begin helping the afflicted, Isaiah says, "The Lord will guide you continually, and satisfy your need in parched places, and make your bones strong; and you shall be like a watered garden, like a spring of water, whose waters never fail." It takes a balance of worship to God and service to others. Judah must take care of their people and they must continue crying out to God. God will hear them and respond with refreshing waters and will restore their ruins.

In South Korea after the professor's lecture, we spoke with our tour guide who had spent a semester studying at Columbia Theological Seminary, so some of us already knew her. She said that while she was studying at our seminary, she noticed the different ministry models within the American church and the Korean church. She had a conversation about this with one of our professors who was a Korean-American. He had observed the differences between our churches as well and offered this insight: some churches focus heavily on charity and justice but are weak in Biblical knowledge and familiarity with the scriptures. He called these churches "the fruits." Then he said there are other churches that focus on Biblical education and building up numbers within the congregation but aren't as active in the outside world. He called these types of churches "the roots." While both types of churches have their strengths, both fruits and roots are necessary to complete the church. Once again, our perceived complexities threaten to cloud our vision. In a busy world when we find it difficult to fit in one worship service a week, we struggle to find time and motivation to balance our churches.

The answer to finding this balance is within this scripture passage itself: "Is it not to share your bread with the hungry, and bring the homeless poor into your house; when you see the naked, to cover them, and not to hide yourself from your own kin?" The people of Judah are all kin. Here the Hebrew word *umibesereka* that has been translated as "kin," literally means "from your own flesh." The hungry, the homeless, the naked are all part of the family of Judah, all from the same flesh. To be considered righteous the people of Judah had a responsibility to take care of their kin. Just as the sin of Judah is corporate and is something that they must all answer to, their repentance must also be corporate. In order to be considered righteous and for their voices to be heard on high, they must embrace their entire community as one family. This is what Isaiah says will raise up the foundations of many generations. Relationships with one another, realizing all people are of the same flesh, are the key to a relationship with God.

As I stated before, the most meaningful part of visiting South Korea was meeting so many of my siblings in Christ. We discovered that several of the people we met had a connection to Columbia though professional relationships and study abroad opportunities. These were our people! We were all so closely connected, our ministries were intertwined, and we didn't even know it until we traveled to the other side of the world. We were kin, of the same flesh. Each pastor and professor we met gave us gifts, provided tea and coffee, welcomed our questions, and reminded us to enjoy ourselves and our ministries. We were treated like family and welcomed with joy at each of our destinations. We even visited a local Anglican cathedral and convent, and one of the nuns blew kisses to us as we left, promising us a room in the convent guest house should we ever like to visit again. The people of South Korea showed me that we are all family. We are all God's children, created in God's image, all of the same flesh. We all belong to one another. We are all responsible for one another.

That revelation in and of itself is what takes the complexity out of our lives. We are all kin, all of the same flesh. If our priority is serving God and serving people, then our churches will be balanced between fruits and roots and the rest of our lives should fall into place. Author Rachel Held Evans shares a story in her book *Faith Unraveled* of her travels in India that exemplifies one way of showing up in the world and learning how to treat strangers like family. In Hyderabad she met a widow named Laxmi who worked at local boarding school. Her husband had died from AIDS, so she and her children were left in poverty. They also tested positive for HIV. A local Christian family had provided Laxmi housing. They saw that her children were denied education for having HIV, so they opened a boarding school for her children and other children who were in similar situations. Laxmi and her children would have been considered untouchable outcasts within the caste system, but this group of Christians took them in and provided for their needs and helped them work for a better future. Rachel says, "So many Christians choose to live in slums and among people suffering from leprosy, to take in the HIV-positive and the disabled, and to give generously to the poor. They subject themselves to poverty and earn reputations for associating with the lower castes." Rachel learned that the church in India brought people into their own homes and provided clothing, education, and food for anyone in need, to the point of being in poverty themselves. These people truly represent what Isaiah asks of the people of Judah by bowing their heads like a bulrush and lying in sackcloth and ashes. One would think that the complexity of the caste system would distract them from taking care of those who are in poverty, but these people see past the caste system and turn it completely upside to show the love of God.

Let us learn from the corporate sin of Judah and take this charge to work together as a corporate body, as one family, so that our voices may be heard on high. If our lives are buried in our own complexities, then or worship only serves our self-interests; but if we awaken the power within our grasp then we can truly affect change in our own communities and around the world. If we follow these commands to humble ourselves, to break the bonds of injustice, to take away the yoke of oppression, to stop pointing fingers, and to stop speaking evil, then God will water us like a garden, allowing us to bear both fruits and roots, which are our actions and our worship. If we share our bread, bring the poor into our house, and cover the naked, then we are serving our kin, our own flesh. Each person we encounter is our family, created in the image of God, and we are responsible for one another. This is what we understand to be true worship. And if we take the time to work on this now, then the light that rises out of the darkness will raise the foundation of many generations. God is poised, listening, ready to respond with "Here I am" should we call out in need of help for this mission. Isaiah tells us that healing will spring up quickly. We are empowered to use all we have been given to serve others and glorify God. With the God of light on our side, it makes things a little less complex.

Return
Joel 2:1-2, 12-17

Blow the trumpet in Zion;
 sound the alarm on my holy mountain!
Let all the inhabitants of the land tremble,
 for the day of the Lord is coming, it is near—
a day of darkness and gloom,
 a day of clouds and thick darkness!
Like blackness spread upon the mountains
 a great and powerful army comes;
their like has never been from of old,
 nor will be again after them
 in ages to come.

Yet even now, says the Lord,
 return to me with all your heart,
with fasting, with weeping, and with mourning;
 rend your hearts and not your clothing.
Return to the Lord, your God,
 for he is gracious and merciful,
slow to anger, and abounding in steadfast love,
 and relents from punishing.
Who knows whether he will not turn and relent,
 and leave a blessing behind him,
a grain offering and a drink offering
 for the Lord, your God?

Blow the trumpet in Zion;
 sanctify a fast;
call a solemn assembly;
 gather the people.
Sanctify the congregation;

assemble the aged;
gather the children,
  even infants at the breast.
Let the bridegroom leave his room,
  and the bride her canopy.

Between the vestibule and the altar
  let the priests, the ministers of the Lord, weep.
Let them say, "Spare your people, O Lord,
  and do not make your heritage a mockery,
  a byword among the nations.
Why should it be said among the peoples,
  'Where is their God?'"

My husband and I celebrated our fifth wedding anniversary in Montreal, Quebec. We rented a townhouse through AirBnb where a kind woman lived and was enjoying her retirement. She was extremely hospitable and was clearly looking for some conversation and to be kept company. When we would return in the evenings, she liked hearing about the parts of the city we had explored that day, but she also really wanted someone to listen to her as well. She told me about how she had lived in the country of Colombia for 15 years, and she regretted moving back to Canada. She had lived in a small, isolated village that was only accessible by boat, but she knew and loved all of the people in the village. They had all taken it upon themselves to care for one another by visiting each other daily and sharing all that they had with one another. She knew that if she moved back to Colombia that she would be giving up the great healthcare, her comfortable living situation, cooler temperatures, and public transportation, but she wanted to return to Colombia because she felt connected and cared for. She wanted to return home.

In this scripture passage we see that repentance returns us home to God. An enemy was coming to invade the land, and the prophet Joel was calling out to the people of Jerusalem to mourn, lament, repent, and gather into the temple to plead with God for protection. This was their home that was being threatened, and they needed help. Darkness, doom, and gloom are described in this prophecy as impending danger closes in. However, Joel called for all people to return to God and rely on the promise of God's restoration for the land and the people. The Hebrew word for "repent" is *shuv*, which means to turn away or return. While the physical home of the people of Jerusalem was being threatened, they knew that God would be their home and their help; to repent or to turn away from their sin, would be to return home to their shelter in God. It's not clear what specific sins that the people needed to repent of in this passage, and it's not stated who the invading enemy was. Those topics are not the emphasis of this prophecy. The important message for the audience to understand about Joel's declaration was that they needed to return to God because they knew that God is merciful and abounding in steadfast love. They were being instructed to fully give themselves over to lament and worship so that God would hear them and respond, just as God has done in days past. In these prophetic books there is always mercy intertwined with judgement.

Since we aren't informed about the sin that the people of Jerusalem had committed, our focus is directed to the consequences of sin. Pastor Morgan Guyton writes about sinfulness and repentance in his article on the Patheos blog, saying, "Many American Christians today operate with a very diminished understanding of sin as mere rule-breaking and insubordination. Sin describes the oppressive weight of every deformity of human relations in our world." Sinfulness is less about displeasing God with every wrong decision we make, and more about the ripple effects of our choices that lead to a world full of pain, suffering, injustice, rage, and hate. In scripture we learn that it's not about God sitting above and taking a tally of our rights and wrongs, but the anger and mourning God feels when our sins, as the human race, create an oppressive world that distances us from God's will. Repentance is an acknowledgment of remorse for making decisions that hurt God's world. Returning to God is returning to peace and reconciliation. We are remorseful because this earth belongs to God, and one day heaven will come down to earth to be our new home.

Pastor Morgan continues on in this article to say, "When I put ashes on my forehead, I'm not saying, 'Look at me, I'm a shiny happy Christian, don't you wish you were as awesome as I am?' I'm saying the world today is unacceptable and I am responsible for my part in creating it... I am not merely responsible for not intentionally breaking God's rules or hurting other people. As one who has received the mercy of God, I am responsible for *being* the mercy of God in the world. The world that Jesus is seeking to create is a world where everyone walks with the world's crucified so that their crucifixion will stop." On Ash Wednesday we enter into a season of repentance not because we are God's bad children who need to be punished, but because God is our help and wants us to live in a home where all people are loved fully. There is a longing in our hearts to be at home and at peace, and we know we are not there yet. God is coming to make our world God's Kingdom, and Joel reminds us that God has always been faithful and merciful in times past. We can trust that God is coming to make all things new and to make this world a new creation where we are at home. Returning to God and repenting of our sins means that we are committing ourselves to fighting against the evil in our hearts and in the world around us so that one day the longing to be home with God will be fulfilled.

We are invited into repentance on this Ash Wednesday so that we might return to God, because God is gracious and is abounding in steadfast love. We are invited to return home to our shelter in God. As we take these ashes, we are turning away from our sin and returning to God's will. That means we do more than say we are sorry for our sin, we are also committing to making a change in our lives to prepare for when God makes all things new. I leave you with this poem by Langston Hughes called, *I Dream a World*. Listen to this poem as it illuminates the kind of home that we long for, and the kind of home that repentance returns us to:

"I dream a world where man// No other man will scorn,// Where love will bless the earth// And peace its paths adorn// I dream a world where all// Will know sweet freedom's way,// Where greed no longer saps the soul// Nor avarice blights our day.// A world I dream where black or white,// Whatever race you be,// Will share the bounties of the earth// And every man is free,// Where wretchedness will hang its head// And joy, like a pearl,// Attends the needs of all mankind-// Of such I dream, my world!"

A Conversation Between Malachi and Paul
Malachi 3:1-4; 1 Corinthians 13:1-3, 11-13

Malachi 3:1-4

See, I am sending my messenger to prepare the way before me, and the Lord whom you seek will suddenly come to his temple. The messenger of the covenant in whom you delight--indeed, he is coming, says the LORD of hosts. But who can endure the day of his coming, and who can stand when he appears? For he is like a refiner's fire and like fullers' soap; he will sit as a refiner and purifier of silver, and he will purify the descendants of Levi and refine them like gold and silver, until they present offerings to the LORD in righteousness. Then the offering of Judah and Jerusalem will be pleasing to the LORD as in the days of old and as in former years.

1 Corinthians 13:1-3, 11-13

If I speak in the tongues of mortals and of angels, but do not have love, I am a noisy gong or a clanging cymbal. And if I have prophetic powers, and understand all mysteries and all knowledge, and if I have all faith, so as to remove mountains, but do not have love, I am nothing. If I give away all my possessions, and if I hand over my body so that I may boast, but do not have love, I gain nothing. When I was a child, I spoke like a child, I thought like a child, I reasoned like a child; when I became an adult, I put an end to childish ways. For now we see in a mirror, dimly, but then we will see face to face. Now I know only in part; then I will know fully, even as I have been fully known. And now faith, hope, and love abide, these three; and the greatest of these is love.

First and foremost, I want to stress that these two texts are unrelated to one another. They were written for different people in a different time. The Malachi text is a prophetic message to the Israelites after the exile when they were allowed to worship together in their homeland again. The letter to the Corinthians is addressing a diverse congregation established as a church of Jesus Christ with prominent members and members of a lower social class. Malachi's text is before the Messiah, while Paul's letter is after Christ has died, resurrected, and has been ascended into heaven for quite some time. But both passages are challenging the audience, pushing them to grow, and making them uncomfortable so that all who hear might be transformed into a more just and loving community that glorifies God. This is why I have put them in conversation with one another, to examine the similarities and differences between Malachi's and Paul's calling for transformation. We are inviting a prophet and an apostle to sit down together and discuss what is required of their audience to honor God. Imagine if you will, these two meeting together to discuss the problems they are facing and how they might address their communities. They are crossing space and time to speak to each other face to face, as friends and colleagues.

In this conversation Malachi might take a seat across a table from Paul and stare down into his coffee deep in thought. Paul would wait patiently as Malachi gathered his thoughts, knowing how hard it is to speak difficult truths. After taking a deep breath, Malachi would begin by telling Paul about the mess that he and his people are in now that they are no longer exiled. They are dealing with the trauma of homelessness and displacement, while struggling to find their identity as God's people. Just as they have suffered, their worship to God has suffered. Their grain offerings and burnt offerings are not the best that they have to offer, and now God is sending a messenger to set them straight. At this moment Malachi might pause and rub his temples. He's frustrated and exhausted. He has compassion for his people, and he's dealing with his own trauma! This is such a heavy load to bear. So, Paul might reach out and give Malachi an encouraging pat on the hand. Malachi would continue on, saying that the day of the Lord is coming! This is good news because that means God is coming to restore the people of Israel. But God's presence is overwhelming. If God is coming to be among them who can truly stand before the awesome, terrible, encompassing presence of God? If God is going to transform God's people, then that means they're going to be judged and changed before being made good. Such a powerful transformation will not be comfortable. In fact, it will likely be painful.

Malachi would then sit back in his chair and shake his head. Paul would nod vigorously and agree. Paul knows what it's like for God to speak from the heavens and transform him completely changing his whole identity down to his name. He's well aware of what God's judgement, although it leads to goodness, really means. So, Paul might take a quick sip of his coffee, and begin telling of the letter he has to send to the church in Corinth. You see, this city has so much promise and potential for spreading the good news of Jesus. Corinth was diverse in culture, ethnicity, and in economic trade. Most of the congregation were Gentiles, which meant the message of Jesus was truly reaching the hearts and minds of new people. This church could really reflect the diversity of God's kingdom! But diversity meant that not everyone had the same social standing and economic income. There were prominent members of means and comfort, while there were also people who were just barely getting by. Paul had emphasized that all people were important to God and had gifts to offer, but the people who had fewer worldly possessions were being treated as less essential to the church. They were being excluded from all the meals and celebrations of the church because they couldn't afford to bring food to share. Their spiritual gifts weren't being used to bless the church. Paul might take a moment to pause to put his head in his hands. Malachi would stand up, squeeze Paul's shoulder and pour him some fresh coffee. Paul would take a sip of his coffee and tell Malachi that if Christians act without love, then it's all just noise. If the church has faith but doesn't have love, then it's all nothing.

At this point the two men might take a moment to sit in silence and share a knowing look. This look communicates their desire to honor God, their compassion for their communities, and their frustration with how hard it is to be a leader. Paul would then stand up to stretch his legs and lean against the window. Malachi would stare out the window too, reclining in his seat. He would then tell Paul that as exciting as it is that the day of the Lord is coming, it will be a day of refining fire and fuller's soap. It will be a day of purification. Being cleansed means checking into habits, being self-reflective of flaws, admitting that there is room for growth and change, and really tearing away all the darkness that's bound to one's soul. Are the people of Israel really ready to sacrifice parts of themselves for the sake of the transformation that God brings? Even Malachi himself, a prophet, may have doubts about the pain of transformation and the sacrifice that it takes. Malachi would take a break to stretch and take a sip of his coffee. He would then stand up and grab some cheese and crackers from the kitchen counter and set them on the table.

Paul might sit down and finish his cup of coffee. Then he and Malachi would grab some crackers and cheese and munch on them quietly for a while. Paul then would say that people can do mighty acts of faith, they can give away their possessions and even sacrifice their bodies for the sake of Jesus Christ, but if all of these great faith acts are done without any love then there is nothing to gain from it. The church falls apart without love and the church of Corinth is truly struggling to show love to one another! Honestly, the way that they treat people who are rich and have a high social standing as more important than anyone else is childish. Paul would then stand up suddenly, very frustrated, knocking over Malachi's coffee. How could these people act like children, reason like children, and speak like children? It's time for them to set aside their childish ways! The future of the church is at stake! Paul would then see the mess he made and grab some napkins to help clean up. Malachi wouldn't be angry. Instead he would agree that all people are made in God's image and deserve to be treated with dignity and respect. God calls all to share what they have with one another, instead of making powerful people even more powerful and impoverished people even more oppressed.

And then as the two are mopping up the spilled coffee together, it would click. They would look up each other and nod, coming to an understanding. Both had different people in different circumstances that they would be addressing, but there was an inescapable similarity that both of these messages contained. God's judgement is never separate from God's mercy. There is always a way to repent and turn back to God. Malachi was talking *to all* the Israelites so that their nation would be restored *as a whole*. Paul was emphasizing the need of unity within the congregation in Corinth so that people in all social classes would be treated with love, honor, and dignity. In both of these scenarios the people of Israel and the church of Corinth needed to be redeemed as a community. Their faith in God was inseparable from their responsibility to love and serve the people around them. Just like Malachi and Paul were cleaning up their coffee mess together, they knew their communities had to work together as a unit, not as individuals, to clean up their messes. Malachi says that this would make the offering of Jerusalem pleasing to God, just like in the days of old. Paul would agree and say that while it's hard for the church to understand this because they see through a mirror dimly, they would soon fully know that the greatest out of faith, hope, and love is, in fact, love.

Then two men would be feeling a little more light-hearted, ready to speak to their communities about the hard truths, and the good news that come from God. After they cleaned up the kitchen, the two would share a handshake and a pat on the back and go their separate ways to do God's work. Malachi would go to prophesy to Israel, telling them that God's judgment is coming, and it's not going to feel good; but if they are willing to withstand transformation then God will restore them. Paul would go to write his letter to Corinth, telling them that they must love each other fully with their whole hearts or else it undercuts all the good and faithful work that they do as a church. And both are going to tell their communities that they have to work together, serving one another. It's not just about a personal relationship between an individual and the Creator of the universe; a relationship with God is inseparable from relationships with others. Now as we come back to our time, our place, and our congregation we have been fortunate enough to overhear this conversation between a prophet and an apostle. Since we have had an inside look and picked the brains of our ancestors, let us learn from the mistakes of the faith communities past, and move forward into a loving, refined future.

A Story from Mary
Matthew 2:13-23

Now after they had left, an angel of the Lord appeared to Joseph in a dream and said, "Get up, take the child and his mother, and flee to Egypt, and remain there until I tell you; for Herod is about to search for the child, to destroy him." Then Joseph got up, took the child and his mother by night, and went to Egypt, and remained there until the death of Herod. This was to fulfill what had been spoken by the Lord through the prophet, "Out of Egypt I have called my son." When Herod saw that he had been tricked by the wise men, he was infuriated, and he sent and killed all the children in and around Bethlehem who were two years old or under, according to the time that he had learned from the wise men. Then was fulfilled what had been spoken through the prophet Jeremiah: "A voice was heard in Ramah, wailing and loud lamentation, Rachel weeping for her children; she refused to be consoled, because they are no more." When Herod died, an angel of the Lord suddenly appeared in a dream to Joseph in Egypt and said, "Get up, take the child and his mother, and go to the land of Israel, for those who were seeking the child's life are dead." Then Joseph got up, took the child and his mother, and went to the land of Israel. But when he heard that Archelaus was ruling over Judea in place of his father Herod, he was afraid to go there. And after being warned in a dream, he went away to the district of Galilee. There he made his home in a town called Nazareth, so that what had been spoken through the prophets might be fulfilled, "He will be called a Nazorean."

Today our sermon will be told from the voice of Mary, the mother of Jesus. Listen to Mary's words to hear a word from God:

Raising a child is an exhausting enough task on its own; raising a child that the governors of our land want to destroy is grueling. But my sweet boy was worth every harrowing journey that we took as refugees seeking a haven from the powers that be. I had said yes to God when tasked with the mission to bear Jesus and raise him. And that's what saying yes to God means: risking life, comfort, safety, and security to fulfill a larger purpose that reveals God's love and justice to the world. Since agreeing to this mission, God has guided every step of the way, sending my family angelic escorts as our companions. So, when the angel came to my husband, Joseph, in a dream instructing us to flee because King Herod sought Jesus' life, our feet were swift with urgency. We wrapped Jesus up tight, gathered a precious few belongings, and whisked away under the cloak of night.

Joseph directed us to Egypt, with pure grit and determination, as I held onto Jesus and looked up to the stars. The stars were our steady constant in this transient life. The cosmos swirled above, evidence of God's sovereignty. Just as they had guided the Wise Men to visit us not so long ago, they shone brightly now breaking through the oppressive darkness. Breathing steadily against my chest was little Jesus, blissfully ignorant of the bounty on his head. I leaned down to kiss his crown and it still smelled sweetly of that enchanting baby smell. Suddenly, I was overcome with awe; to think that I had been entrusted to care for Emmanuel. The king of the Jews was fully dependent on me. My body had housed him, nourishing him as he grew strong and ready to enter the world. And now he depends upon my milk for sustenance and my arms for shelter. My mothering love was essential to his survival upon this earth, and I was willing to offer my body completely and wholly to protect him. Upon this revelation, I shared a meager smile with Joseph, who unfurrowed his brow and squeezed my hand in return as we traversed onward.

We arrived in Egypt, safe from the grasping fingers of death's reach. However, while we remained in safety, I received word that countless other families were preyed upon by the power-hungry king. Leaving didn't end the problem, but only reinforced it. The Wise Men had protected our whereabouts, but this only infuriated King Herod, who took his wrath to the homes of Bethlehem and slaughtered all of the children in and around the city who were two years old or younger. When I heard the news, I recalled the words from Jeremiah, "A voice was heard in Ramah, wailing and loud lamentation, Rachel weeping for her children; she refused to be consoled, because they are no more." While I couldn't audibly hear the wails of the mothers of Bethlehem, I heard them in my heart. We had worked so hard to protect Jesus that I could just imagine the searing pain ripping through the hearts of the mothers. I grabbed Jesus up and held him close. I wept for gratefulness, I wept for grief, and I wept for guilt. I was so thankful that my child had been spared, but I hurt for the other mothers. And I could not help but feel deep and shameful guilt, feeling as if I were to blame for this massacre of the infants.

Joseph returned home after a long day of work to find me huddled on the floor in tears. He had also heard the news, so I didn't need to explain what had happened. He sat down next to me and wrapped me and Jesus in his arms. After a moment I released Jesus who had been fussing and squirming so that he could go back to playing. I confessed my guilt to Joseph. He reminded me of all the signs we had received until this point. We had been sent the angels, the shepherds, the Wise Men, and we had witnessed all of the miraculous events leading to the birth of Jesus. Joseph said that these were evidence that our mission is God-given, and every step we had taken had been divinely appointed. We had the host of angels on our side and the fate of our people depended on our task to raise the

Messiah. I realized that we stand in solidarity with the suffering and the oppressed by feeling their pain and working toward a better future. By answering God's call to raise Jesus, we were participating in God's justice for the downtrodden. Joseph and I sat in silence for a while, and I breathed in peace and exhaled the guilt and shame. I knew that Jesus' coming into the world was meant to do that: allow us the peace that banishes guilt.

Suddenly, an angel of the Lord appeared to Joseph in a dream and told him that Herod had died. We were to go back to Israel where we would finally be safe. The news of Herod's death rippled through the land and brought great joy! Those who had been devastated by the horrific bloodshed brought by his hands could finally find closure and healing. However, this meant that we had to traverse the land again, embarking on another long, hard journey with only what we could carry on our backs. On the wings of angels and by the twinkle of stars we moved our weary bones back to Israel. But just as we arrived, we heard that Archelaus, the son of Herod, had risen to power in Judea. We were afraid that he would continue his father's legacy of viciously seeking the life of Jesus. We were uncertain as to what to do next. God confirmed our suspicions and warned Joseph in a dream that staying would bring disaster.

One more journey. One more flight. Jesus was getting big and heavy. He was crawling and climbing, becoming adventurous and wanting to explore the world around him. He needed a safe place to investigate his surroundings, to play, to imagine, to grow tall, and to become a man. One last time we gathered our belongings, not even having to plan or consider what to take and leave behind. We had become very skilled at packing and moving. But we knew this was right and necessary. We were saying yes to God again, and we would keep saying yes to the ends of the earth if it meant that Jesus' future would be fulfilled. It was time to leave once more and hopefully settle down.

When deciding where to go next, we recalled the words of the prophets speaking about the Messiah saying, "He will be called a Nazorean." So, we settled in the district of Galilee in the city of Nazareth. We hoped that this is where we would find sanctuary, where we would build a home and a life, where we would be integrated into the community, and where we would grow our family. This is where we desired to find peace. Perhaps this would be the hometown where Jesus could claim as his own and begin his ministry. Jesus of Nazareth.

So, this is what saying "yes" to God looks like. Leaving all that is familiar, being uprooted, moving when you're tired, and traveling when you want to settle. Saying a "yes" once does not suffice, but there must be a new "yes" with each new task. But with sacrifice comes great reward. I was the first to know of the good news of the Messiah. I was the first to carry that good news. I was the first to have Jesus in my heart because I had him in my womb. And I was the one who delivered the good news into the world. The cries of the mothers robbed of their children still ring in my ears, but when I look into the eyes of wild little Jesus, I know that the infants were not forgotten and forsaken. All who have suffered will receive the justice that they hunger for when this mighty boy grows up. As Joseph and I rest our travel worn bodies, we share a knowing smile that when heaven and earth meet it's a messy chaos that ultimately ends in joy. Perhaps life will be uneventful for a while. We may even live as normal, average people raising a little family for a few years. Living the extraordinary is breathtaking and exhausting, and we have been chosen to participate in God's mighty purpose for Jesus. We don't know what other exciting, heartbreaking challenges will face us next, but when God calls down from heaven, we have committed to continue saying yes, yes, and yes.

Jesus Abandoned
Matthew 27:45-56

From noon on, darkness came over the whole land until three in the afternoon. And about three o'clock Jesus cried with a loud voice, "Eli, Eli, lema sabachthani?" that is, "My God, my God, why have you forsaken me?" When some of the bystanders heard it, they said, "This man is calling for Elijah." At once one of them ran and got a sponge, filled it with sour wine, put it on a stick, and gave it to him to drink. But the others said, "Wait, let us see whether Elijah will come to save him." Then Jesus cried again with a loud voice and breathed his last. At that moment the curtain of the temple was torn in two, from top to bottom. The earth shook, and the rocks were split. The tombs also were opened, and many bodies of the saints who had fallen asleep were raised. After his resurrection they came out of the tombs and entered the holy city and appeared to many. Now when the centurion and those with him, who were keeping watch over Jesus, saw the earthquake and what took place, they were terrified and said, "Truly this man was God's Son!" Many women were also there, looking on from a distance; they had followed Jesus from Galilee and had provided for him. Among them were Mary Magdalene, and Mary the mother of James and Joseph, and the mother of the sons of Zebedee.

Today is Palm Sunday, also known as Passion Sunday. Today we remember Jesus' triumphant entry into Jerusalem surrounded by waving palm branches and the echoes of loud Hosannas. But the tension of Palm Sunday is that the celebration balances on the cusp of the inevitable tragedy that is to come: Christ's death, the Passion story. A common theme seen throughout the Passion story is abandonment. Jesus is betrayed by Judas, who exposes him for a handful of silver that he doesn't even want. Jesus is abandoned by the rest of the disciples by the end of the night. Most notably, Jesus is abandoned by Peter, who denies him three times and immediately regrets it. And yet Peter doesn't right his wrong but stays silent and protected from being associated with the Messiah. Jesus is deserted by Pilate, the one who condemns him. Pilate cowers, gives into the crowds, and washes his hands, refusing to take accountability for the sentencing, hiding behind the anger of the crowds, dodging responsibility. According to the Gospel of Mathew even the other two criminals on the cross, who were in the same situation as Jesus, taunted him. Finally, Jesus cries out to God, questioning why he had been forsaken.

Jesus had seemingly been abandoned by all. But there were some who stood in solidarity, who were present through the death, the burial, and the resurrection. After Jesus dies, it is revealed in Matthew 27:55 that many women were present at the crucifixion, looking from afar. In verse 61 two of those women who were present, Mary Magdalene and Mary the mother of James and Joseph, go to bury the body. They didn't abandon Jesus but stayed through the blood-soaked death and burial when everyone else had fled. They stood in solidarity, remaining with Jesus through the suffering, despite the possible peril it might have put them in for being associated with him. They threw caution to the wind when it came their own well-being so that they could love and support Jesus. As women, they had limited influence in society with which they could stop the events from happening, so they offered themselves, their presence, their hands, their feet, their eyes, their very lives to stand against the injustice that Jesus was suffering. Then in chapter 28, Mary Magdalene and the other Mary went to the tomb and were present to see the glory of the resurrection of Christ. They survived the risky, compassionate choice to stand in solidarity and were the ones who were able to witness the ultimate victory.

As we relive this passion story, how can we translate these events to today? Jesus is not physically among us, so how do we refuse to abandon Jesus and dare to stand in solidarity with him? Not long before his death, Jesus says that when judgment comes, he will take note of those who took care of the least of these. Those who are strangers, hungry, thirsty, sick, naked, and in prison are who Jesus describes as the least of these. Jesus says what you do for the least of these, you do for me. When we take care of our neighbor, when we stand in solidarity with them, we are serving Jesus. If we ignore them, call them names, exclude them, make laws or repeal laws that further oppress them, then we are abandoning Jesus. In the spirit of the passion story, let us learn from those who abandoned Jesus so that we may not be like them. We have many neighbors who look different than us, who speak different languages from us. Let us dare to call them "beloved" instead of "illegal." We have teenagers on the streets who have been kicked out of their homes due to sexual orientation or pregnancy out of wedlock. Let us dare to call them "children of God" instead of "disappointments." We have over 10,000 homeless people in the Atlanta area who are hungry and who are thirsty. Let us call them "claimed" instead of "leeches." If we strip away all of our preconceived notions and are able to see Jesus in each person, we are refusing to be the abandoners of the passion and claiming to be those who stand in solidarity of the resurrection. There are needs to be met out in the world, and the story of Jesus calls us out of our homes and out of our pews to meet them where they are.

Mary Magdalene and the other Mary bore witness to the glory of the resurrection. Next week, we're going to celebrate it loud and proud. And we get to look forward to the second coming of Christ, the one that we all get to bask in. When Christ returns, will he see us as those who stood in solidarity with him? Will we be like the women of the passion story? We can learn what the pain of abandonment looks like from this story and look forward to the glory that comes in solidarity. We cannot hide from all that is scary or ugly or threatening in the world. We must be willing to offer ourselves in the face of injustice. Our presence and persistence against the darkness is what will lead us to God's encompassing light. Our hearts are heavy this week as we relive the death of our Savior. But let's lean into that darkness and that pain, because the light is coming. Let this open our eyes to the darkness around us so that we can be sparks of this coming light.

Perplexed and Pondering
Luke 1:26-38

In the sixth month the angel Gabriel was sent by God to a town in Galilee called Nazareth, to a virgin engaged to a man whose name was Joseph, of the house of David. The virgin's name was Mary. And he came to her and said, "Greetings, favored one! The Lord is with you." But she was much perplexed by his words and pondered what sort of greeting this might be.

The angel said to her, "Do not be afraid, Mary, for you have found favor with God. And now, you will conceive in your womb and bear a son, and you will name him Jesus. He will be great, and will be called the Son of the Most High, and the Lord God will give to him the throne of his ancestor David. He will reign over the house of Jacob forever, and of his kingdom there will be no end." Mary said to the angel, "How can this be, since I am a virgin?" The angel said to her, "The Holy Spirit will come upon you, and the power of the Most High will overshadow you; therefore the child to be born will be holy; he will be called Son of God. And now, your relative Elizabeth in her old age has also conceived a son; and this is the sixth month for her who was said to be barren. For nothing will be impossible with God." Then Mary said, "Here am I, the servant of the Lord; let it be with me according to your word." Then the angel departed from her.

Year in and year out we celebrate Advent and Christmas. We know all about the angels, the virgin, the manger, the baby, the star, the shepherds, and the wise men. We know all the special buzzwords like Bethlehem, the stable, gold, frankincense and myrrh, glory to God in the highest. We put on our mismatched hand sewn costumes of tunics and head coverings and we perform the story in our hand built stable that fits neatly at the front of the church with enough straw to lie cleanly in the manger so as not to sully the church carpet. If we want to get truly adventurous, we might even have a real baby in swaddling clothes, and maybe a live donkey and sheep in an outdoor nativity scene. The story of Jesus' birth has become very familiar. We know it by heart. Since we know it so well that we can retell it by memory, sometimes I find that we have ceased our wonder and marvel of such an unimaginable story. We skip right to the nativity without sitting with Mary as she is perplexed by the words of the angel and ponders what all of this news means. We get antsy if we're not singing Christmas carols during Advent, instead of leaning into the anticipation and expectation. Then we're ready to take the tree down as soon as Christmas day is over, because by the time it gets here we're all partied out! Instead of waiting, expecting, and pondering in Advent, and then celebrating Christmas for 12 days, it seems like we're dragging out Christmas. What's really happening is that we don't have the patience to wait for it so that it might be celebrated properly. How can we celebrate with jubilation if we didn't have to first long for something to celebrate? How do we know we are ready for the Christ child if we do not take time to sit with Mary and be perplexed and ponder this great mystery with her?

I, like many of you, have more than one nativity scene in my home. I want a visual reminder of what Christmas is about and what we've been waiting for during all of Advent. But in our rush to the manger, we forget all the wild events that led to the birth of Jesus, the grit and surprise of the birth, and the terror that followed. Our mantel piece nativity scenes are a wonderful reminder, but they are just that: a reminder. They do not contain the whole of the Gospel, and sometimes I fear that we've tamed the Gospel as if it's a children's fairytale. In fact, let's visit a popular fairytale that shows us an infinite God that cannot be contained and breaks through the barriers of heaven and earth.

In C.S. Lewis' children's story, *The Lion, the Witch, and the Wardrobe*, four siblings Lucy, Edmund, Susan, and Peter enter an old wardrobe into a magical world known as Narnia. Here they meet magical creatures that can speak, like Mr. Tumnus who is a faun, half man and half goat. The world of Narnia is stuck in an eternal winter as cursed by the White Witch, who is evil and powerful. The White Witch wants to capture these four children for fear that they will overthrow her from her throne, and she arrests Mr. Tumnus for helping them instead of turning them over to the authorities. Mr. and Mrs. Beaver, who are two talking beavers as we learn that the animals in Narnia can speak, decide to help the four children find Mr. Tumnus and set other prisoners free from the White Witch. The Beavers are excited and confident in their mission because they know that Aslan is coming. Aslan is a lion and the King of Narnia. The Beavers know that Aslan the King can save everyone from the White Witch and the eternal winter plaguing Narnia. The children are a little concerned, wondering if this lion that they don't know is dangerous. Susan asks if Aslan is safe, and Mrs. Beaver says that anyone who doesn't approach Aslan with knees knocking is a fool. Lucy then says that he mustn't be a safe lion. Mr. Beaver says that of course he isn't safe, but he is the King and he is good. Aslan indeed comes as a metaphorical Christ figure to save the day and overcome the death and evil that has choked Narnia for so long.

Just as Aslan is good and a savior, but cannot be assumed to be safe and tame, we too cannot tame the story of the Gospel, forgetting the divine mystery that causes us to be perplexed. What a wild story of a virgin named Mary, who is unexpectedly visited by an angel. With no warning, a heavenly being suddenly appears to her, greeting her as a favored one and being told that the Lord is with her. Well, what on earth does that mean? Is the Lord with everyone or just Mary? And since when did Mary become favored? No wonder she was perplexed! Where is this conversation going? What's about to happen? And then the angel says not to be afraid, when we all know that telling people to calm down doesn't really help anyone calm down. Then Gabriel continues to say that she will conceive a son, name him Jesus, and he will have the throne of his ancestor David. Excuse me, what? *The* David, the man after God's own heart, Jesus will have *that* throne? This is so outlandish! And it's impossible, since Mary is a virgin. Oh wait, no, no, apparently that's not a problem. The Holy Spirit will overshadow her so that she'll conceive, because that happens every day. Oh, and no big deal or anything, but this child will be called the Son of God. There's nothing written in this passage to indicate that time passed for Mary to process this bombshell. But what we do see is something absolutely miraculous: Mary consents. She accepts this task. Regardless of whether she truly comprehended the immensity of the mission set before her, she says, "Let it be." This enormous, breathtaking story gives us an opportunity to pause, to marvel, and to really mull over what this miracle means. We can't truly appreciate the child in the manger, if we blow past this sensation at break-neck speed.

If we lose our wonder and awe, then we lose the essence of what it means to have Emmanuel, God with us. In her book, *Bright Evening Star*, Madeleine L'Engle describes the wonder of Christmas that she had as a child. She would climb into her grandmother's lap at the family beach house, and they would sway back and forth together in the rocking chair on the porch overlooking the sand dunes. Madeleine would feel safe in her grandmother's arms as they watched the waves roll in, and her grandmother would sing about the baby Jesus, the little lamb. This made Madeleine marvel at the Maker of the Universe who would be born in this world to show love for us. Her grandmother would then read her an illustrated picture book about Bible stories, and she believed all of the stories about God's love to be "gloriously true." She pondered this perplexing mystery of Jesus being born into the world, and she poses the question, "Was there a moment, known only to God, when all the stars held their breath, when the galaxies paused in their dance for a fraction of a second, and the Word, who had called it all into being, went with all his love into the womb of a young girl, and the universe started to breathe again, and the ancient harmonies resumed their song, and the angels clapped their hands for joy?" She asks the reader this question because she believes that the story of Christ's coming has become over sentimentalized, and the truth is no longer so striking. Instead of awed silence, we meet the incarnation of Christ with a season of frantic stress, depression, and alienation. Madeleine challenges us to continue to be perplexed by the mystery of the coming of Jesus and ponder on what it means in our hearts so that we do not lose our wonder and awe.

It's the last week of Advent, and Christmas will be here in just a few short days. When we do finally get to Christmas day, let's try not to jump straight to hallelujahs and praises, but pause and continue to be perplexed and pondering. Be perplexed at the God of the universe deciding to enter the world through a woman's womb, covered in afterbirth only to be placed in a manger among barn animals. Ponder what it means for the first people in the world to know about the birth of Christ to be shepherds, people who, in this society, had no power or influence. Let's sit in awe with Mary for a few more days. When we look at the nativity sets on our mantle, let them drive us deeper into the mystery of God instead of letting them be a sentimental, tame fairytale. I leave you with this poem titled *Kneeling Places* by Ann Weems. May it inspire a wonder in your hearts:

"In each heart lies a Bethlehem// An inn where we must ultimately answer// Whether there is room or not.// When we are Bethlehem-bound// We experience our own advent in his.// When we are Bethlehem-bound// We can no longer look the other way// Conveniently not seeing stars// Not hearing angel voices.// We can no longer excuse ourselves by busily// Tending our sheep or our kingdoms.// This advent, let's go to Bethlehem// and see this thing that the Lord has made known to us.// In the midst of shopping sprees // Let's ponder in our hearts the Gift of gifts.// Through the tinsel// Let's look for the gold of the Christmas Star.// In the excitement and confusion, in the merry chaos,// Let's listen for the brush of angel' wings.// This advent let's go to Bethlehem// And find our kneeling places."

Is it Real?
John 1:1-5

In the beginning was the Word, and the Word was with God, and the Word was God. He was in the beginning with God. All things came into being through him, and without him not one thing came into being. What has come into being in him was life, and the life was the light of all people. The light shines in the darkness, and the darkness did not overcome it.

As a preacher's kid I grew up hearing the Gospel and reading scriptures every single day. Sometimes hearing scriptures several times over and interpreted in the same exact way can make passages lose their poignancy and limit understanding. I thought I knew the Gospels backwards and forwards, until I moved to Atlanta for seminary and heard new insights from people of different ethnicities, races, denominations, and sexual orientations. I remember in my first year of seminary I attended a vigil for the numerous shootings of black men and black boys in our nation. We sat in the darkened chapel as the sun was setting with candles in our hands, and this scripture passage was read, "The light shines in the darkness, and the darkness did not overcome it." Suddenly, this passage was real and alive to me in a way that it had never been before. In this moment, as I stared down at the flickering flame in my hand surrounded by the darkness of the chapel, I fully believed the Gospel as I held the truth in my hands. The hope of Jesus Christ was more real than it had ever been before. During this vigil we mourned the evils of racism together as a community, but in the name of Jesus, we proclaimed together that evil and injustice do not have the final word. This scripture passage reminded me of this in a tangible way. The light shines and it will not be overcome. The Gospel is true, I can hold it in my hands. It's real.

That's what this passage from the Gospel according to John is communicating: The Word that was with God and was God became flesh and lived among us. The Word who was God, the Word who was the Father's Son, became visible and tangible to us. The glory of God, full of grace and truth, lived life with us. The Gospel materialized before the eyes of those who saw Jesus, who heard his teaching, who were fed by him, who were healed by his hands. This is how we know that the light shines in the darkness, and the darkness will not overcome it. It has already happened. The darkness has been overcome, not just in the moment when Jesus came, lived, died, and resurrected, *but for all of time.* It's real.

This does not mean that the darkness no longer exists. We know this to be too true. Schools, businesses, concerts, night clubs, and houses of worship have all been targeted by gun violence. Sexual violence is continually covered up to protect powerful people, while the victims are silenced. People who are not native to this country are demonized and treated as invaders to be kept out, instead of being treated with compassion and human dignity. Transgender people are targeted by those who fear and rage against their gender identity. The darkness can be suffocating; the human lives lost to hate means that the darkness is as tangible as the Gospel. The darkness is so overwhelming, but when people of faith come together in love, hope, mourning, and justice, then we are living the prevailing truth of Christ's light. When we, as the church, show up to gently speak love into hurting places, then the light shines in the darkness. Showing up to listen, to pray, to cry, and to protest helps us shine. When we enact the love of Christ, others can see that it's real.

When the light is bright, when the truth takes hold, and when hope is found the fear of the darkness is banished. The darkness may still exist, but we can fight back in the name of Jesus. In a physical sense, darkness can be frightening. Once when my husband and I were going for our daily walk on the beach, the days had been getting shorter and we ended up outside when it was a bit darker. My husband and I like to walk through the water when we are on the beach, but at night we tend to shy away from the water. We can't see anything in the waves, which makes them look menacing. It was impossible to see what creatures might be swimming beneath the surface. But it was a full moon that evening, so taking a walk when it was darker wasn't so bad because we could still see. In fact, with the full moon glistening off the top of the ocean, I couldn't help but be drawn in. I kept walking a little further in the waves, closer to the reflection of the moon. I was wading deeper, unafraid of whatever creatures I couldn't see swarming around me. I just wanted to get as close as I could to the moon's reflection in the water. I was hypnotized by my desire to bathe in the moonlight. Eventually the spell was broken as I was getting wetter and colder, and I reluctantly made my way back to the beach. The shining moonlight made me unafraid of the dark, swirling waves around me. I was not overcome by the darkness but drawn in by the light. We, too, do not have to be afraid because the light of Jesus Christ came walking on the earth. It's real.

If we are to carry the light of Jesus within us, we must be willing to make room for it. That means we strive to let go any of the darkness within our own selves that we might be hiding in. The darkness in the world finds its way into the corners of our hearts. If we engage in challenging ourselves in our spiritual lives and in our personal relationships through prayer, healing, and reconciliation we can confront the pain and sin that accumulates in our souls. This removes all the heavy burdens that hold us back from living an abundant life walking in the grace and love of God. When we make room for light in our own lives by taking the risk of getting messy and making sacrifices, we grow. Our growth makes us more like Christ, the word made flesh. Our growth shows that the Gospel is real.

One summer I held an art camp at a small church for the local children; this church was willing to get messy and make sacrifices for the sake of growth. The church that was hosting the camp had a basement area with a room that had a large, empty wall. They offered this wall for the kids to paint a mural. Since this was a rural area there weren't many summer programs for children, especially affordable ones, so we were offering this week-long program as a free event for kids in the area. This church didn't have any children or families attending, and this camp was an attempt to reach out to that demographic. At the art camp our focus was on this scripture passage, specifically, "The Light shines in the darkness, and the darkness did not overcome it." Nearly 20 kids from the community showed up to play games, eat snacks, paint, and get messy. We had a wonderful time of fellowship and friend making. We spent all week painting the mural on the wall with sources of light: candles, fireflies, constellations, sunsets, and fireworks. Each contribution from the children was special gifts to the whole art piece. Each star, firefly, and candle were unique to the hand of the artist that painted them. In the end, we had a beautiful mural full of light overcoming darkness that 20 kids, who were new to this church, had come together and painted.

Sure, paint found its way onto some places on the floor, and some of the molding on the wall became splattered. They thought they were just sacrificing a wall, but children often color out of the lines. However, this church now has a beautiful artistic creation that they get to enjoy for years to come thanks to the children that they welcomed into their church. They even added a new family with young children as congregation members. For a small church, this is an enormous gain. They were willing to make room for Christ's light, and they grew as a congregation. The Gospel was alive for them that summer, and the light entered the church. It was real.

So now, I leave you with these questions: When you hear that the light shines in the darkness and the darkness did not overcome it, do you believe that it's real? How have you seen the light of Christ in your life? Can you touch it, hold it, make room for it, carry it, and share it? I invite you to take these stories of the light overcoming the darkness and meditate on them. The darkness can be overwhelming and suffocating; although it exists and persists, it never has the final word so long as the light of Christ shines. The darkness has been overcome and will be banished forever. Until then, fear not and know that the light is real.

Empty-Tomb People
John 20:19-31

When it was evening on that day, the first day of the week, and the doors of the house where the disciples had met were locked for fear of the Jews, Jesus came and stood among them and said, "Peace be with you." After he said this, he showed them his hands and his side. Then the disciples rejoiced when they saw the Lord. Jesus said to them again, "Peace be with you. As the Father has sent me, so I send you." When he had said this, he breathed on them and said to them, "Receive the Holy Spirit. If you forgive the sins of any, they are forgiven them; if you retain the sins of any, they are retained." But Thomas (who was called the Twin), one of the twelve, was not with them when Jesus came. So the other disciples told him, "We have seen the Lord." But he said to them, "Unless I see the mark of the nails in his hands, and put my finger in the mark of the nails and my hand in his side, I will not believe." A week later his disciples were again in the house, and Thomas was with them. Although the doors were shut, Jesus came and stood among them and said, "Peace be with you." Then he said to Thomas, "Put your finger here and see my hands. Reach out your hand and put it in my side. Do not doubt but believe." Thomas answered him, "My Lord and my God!" Jesus said to him, "Have you believed because you have seen me? Blessed are those who have not seen and yet have come to believe." Now Jesus did many other signs in the presence of his disciples, which are not written in this book. But these are written so that you may come to believe that Jesus is the Messiah, the Son of God, and that through believing you may have life in his name.

There is a popular comic strip series by Radio Free Babylon called "Coffee with Jesus." It typically depicts a religious person conversing with Jesus over coffee. Sometimes the message is a funny one, and other times it's more profound. Whichever tone it conveys the comic provides thoughts to ponder. I saw a particular panel with a clergy man eagerly leaning in and asking Jesus, "Should I do that graphic, bloody crucifixion description again for the big Easter crowd, Jesus? Really hit 'em with the suffering you endured on our behalf?" Jesus lifts his coffee cup and says, "Not again, Joe, please. They know I suffered. And the people who don't hang out with me don't need some R-rated, gore-fest guilt trip." Joe the clergy man is shocked and protests, saying, "Those very people need a *message*, Jesus! They're there on Christmas and Easter *only*! What do I tell them?" Jesus takes a slow sip of his coffee, then simply says, "Say: *Welcome. Good to see you. How ya been?* The things people say when they haven't seen each other in a while, Joe. And tell them Jesus says 'Hi.'"

As Christians we are known as Easter people, but sometimes it feels as if we only celebrate for one day each year, then we forget about the victory of the resurrection. We find ourselves going right back to the blood-stained cross, which holds all of our sins, guilt, and shame, all of the things that hold us back. Sometimes we find ourselves turning our backs to the empty tomb, similar to Joe the clergyman. I believe that is because the cross is tangible. We can hold it, wrap our hands around it, feel it, and understand it. The cross is what brought Jesus' death, and the finality of death is easy to understand. The restrictions of sin and guilt are easy to understand. As we see in the scripture passage, Thomas understood that Jesus was crucified. Jesus was nailed to the cross and pierced in the side, and that was it. That's the end. Thomas said he will not believe that the disciples have seen the Lord unless he himself sees the mark of the nails in his hands and puts his hand *in* the mark of the nails and *in* his side. There's no way a scarred corpse is walking about, right? Thomas needed something tangible for his faith, too.

The concept of resurrection is much more difficult to comprehend. How can death not be the end? How can we really be set free from sin? Not too long ago I was having a conversation with colleagues and professors, and we were discussing how one of the most popular Christian symbols is a cross; and for denominations that are not Catholic, our symbol is an empty cross. We understand that Jesus didn't stay on the cross. He was resurrected, and yet we still cling to the cross. One of the professors suggested that perhaps a more appropriate symbol would be an empty tomb, since we are Easter people who live this life of resurrection every day. She thought that a better depiction to put on our shirts or wear on necklaces or put on our car bumper stickers would be an empty tomb. I loved this idea and pondered on why we haven't embraced the empty tomb as much as the cross. I realized an empty tomb isn't as easy to grasp as a cross. In an empty tomb we are grabbing at nothing but air. Some may find that scary: we can't grasp the empty tomb, we can't fully understand it, there's nothing physically in there for our faith to cling to, it's not tangible. That, my friends, is the good news. There is nothing, no thing, left in the tomb. No, we cannot hold the empty tomb, and the empty tomb could not hold our Savior.

As we see in this passage, not only could Jesus not be bound by death and the tomb, but he could not be barred by locked doors either. As the disciples were fearfully hiding behind lock and key, Jesus appeared. No knocking on the door or unlocking it with the key, Jesus just appeared. He greeted the disciples with peace, but as we see in the text, they did not respond to this greeting. In fact, the rejoicing and recognition of Jesus didn't come from the disciples until after revealed his scars. While Thomas gets a bad reputation for being the "doubting one" of the group, what we really see is that they were all doubters. Just like Thomas, they needed the scars, something tangible as proof that Jesus Christ was, in fact, alive. The disciples celebrated and Jesus repeated his passing of peace. He said that just as the Father has sent him, he was sending the disciples; but the disciples didn't go anywhere until Jesus breathed the Holy Spirit onto them.

We are like the disciples in that we need tangible objects, too. While we have the cross, we also have the written Gospel. The author even states that these events are written in this book so that we may come to believe that Jesus is the Messiah, the Son of God, and we may have life in his name. We can hold and touch the written account of Christ. Every first Sunday, we celebrate another symbol of Christ: the Eucharist, the Lord's Supper. The broken bread and the poured wine or juice isn't just a tangible symbol of the Gospel, but an ingestible one. And I don't know about you but sometimes I have to have the communion elements to chew, sip, and swallow in order to help me try to grasp at some wisp of understanding of the resurrection. We have these symbols and tools, because sometimes we need something to lay our hands on, to run our fingers over. We so frequently are like Thomas and we have to thrust our hands into some physical evidence. We must do just as Jesus commanded Thomas and reach!

Once the disciples were convinced that Christ had risen, Jesus told the disciples to leave him. Jesus says, "As the Father has sent me, so I send you." While it may have been tempting for the disciples to remain in the presence of the physical evidence of their faith, they had to chase after the invisible Holy Spirit in order to enact this belief and good news. We may need the tangible to hold onto for affirmation, but the essence of our faith comes in the form of an empty tomb and the power of the Holy Spirit breathed onto us from Jesus himself. These are the things we can't see but must trust. "Blessed are those who have not seen and yet have come to believe." The unseen, the untouchable is where the core of our faith is. Jesus wishes peace upon the disciples and tells them to believe. Peace and beliefs are the intangible guides of our faith and are the tenants on which it relies on. What we can hold and touch may be our reassurance, but the empty tomb is what propels us forward in the world. This is because there's nothing for us in an empty tomb, nothing to hold us there; and if we want to find Jesus in the world then we must leave what's empty and go find him.

Clarence Jordan, a farmer and Greek New Testament scholar tells us, "The resurrection of Jesus was simply God's unwillingness to take no for an answer. He raised Jesus, not as an invitation to us to come to heaven when we die, but as a declaration that he himself has now established permanent, eternal residence here on earth. He is standing beside us, strengthening us in this life. The good news of the resurrection of Jesus is not that we shall die and go home to be with him, but that he is risen and comes home with us, bringing all his hungry, naked, thirsty, sick, prisoner brothers with him." While eternal life in heaven is good news, the point of the resurrection is that we have work to do. Jesus is with us in our work, in our daily lives, and most importantly, if we want to see the face of Jesus, we must look into the eyes of those around us.

Jesus says, "If you forgive the sins of any, they are forgiven. If you retain the sins of any, they are retained." Right at this moment, Jesus was giving the disciples some of his power. They were given the power to forgive others, to forgive them of sins. As Jesus taught and worked miracles during his life, he also forgave sins. Now Jesus was commissioning the disciples to do what he had been doing. So, if we, as disciples, use this power to help others understand the forgiveness of sins, we are being witnesses of Jesus to them. "Peace be with you," Christ spoke as a greeting. If we model Jesus in this passage, we notice the peace precedes belief. Jesus spoke peace first and foremost to the disciples and again to Thomas. Then came the physical evidence. Then came belief and the rejoicing, "My Lord, my God!" Like most of us, maybe other people need something tangible before they can believe, too. We do work as peacemakers, peacemakers who meet the needs of the hungry, sick, thirsty, and poor. Unlike Jesus, locked doors may keep us out, but perhaps peace can slip through the cracks, sneak its way through the windows, and squeeze through the keyhole to find the person inside. Maybe if our neighbors can touch our hands, which are acting as the hands of Christ to the world, then those we encounter can believe, too.

What a holy moment for the disciples and Thomas to touch Jesus. We have the honor of being a witness to Jesus to others and enacting that holy moment by offering our hands. In these moments maybe we'll encounter Jesus and touch his hands too. Needing the tangible is not a weakness. Thomas and the other disciples may have been frightened and may have doubted, but Jesus knew that they needed his scars as evidence. We touch so we can understand. But there are things about our faith that we cannot fully understand, or touch, or control. "Blessed are those who have not seen and yet have come to believe." The cross, the scars, the nails, the bread, the wine, are our symbols. But we are Easter people, resurrection people, alleluia people, empty tomb people. Our faith doesn't rely on what we can touch, but the fact that the tomb is empty and there is nothing tangible for us there. The tomb could not hold Jesus in, and that is how we know he is the Messiah, the Son of God, and how we have life in his name. May the nothingness in the tomb set us free and propel us forward.

Children and Heirs
Romans 8:12-25

So then, brothers and sisters, we are debtors, not to the flesh, to live according to the flesh -- for if you live according to the flesh, you will die; but if by the Spirit you put to death the deeds of the body, you will live. For all who are led by the Spirit of God are children of God. For you did not receive a spirit of slavery to fall back into fear, but you have received a spirit of adoption. When we cry, "Abba! Father!" it is that very Spirit bearing witness with our spirit that we are children of God, and if children, then heirs, heirs of God and joint heirs with Christ--if, in fact, we suffer with him so that we may also be glorified with him. I consider that the sufferings of this present time are not worth comparing with the glory about to be revealed to us. For the creation waits with eager longing for the revealing of the children of God; for the creation was subjected to futility, not of its own will but by the will of the one who subjected it, in hope that the creation itself will be set free from its bondage to decay and will obtain the freedom of the glory of the children of God. We know that the whole creation has been groaning in labor pains until now; and not only the creation, but we ourselves, who have the first fruits of the Spirit, groan inwardly while we wait for adoption, the redemption of our bodies. For in hope we were saved. Now hope that is seen is not hope. For who hopes for what is seen? But if we hope for what we do not see, we wait for it with patience.

"For all who are led of the Spirit are the children of God... and if children, then heirs, joint heirs with Christ." These words serve as a reminder of the identity of the individuals in the congregation in Rome, because at this time the church was divided against itself. This church and the message of the

Gospel in Rome were in danger because of the division between the two groups of people within the congregation. The Jewish Christians and the Christian Gentiles had doubts about one another's faith, and Paul was reminding them that they were united as God's children despite previous religious and cultural differences. The truth from this passage still rings all too true for the church today. We're so divided that people have left the church in droves because far too often we're fighting over our differences and losing focus on the Gospel. The creation groans in labor pains for redemption, for the children of God to be revealed. People are hungry for love and belonging, to be known and to be embraced. The message of the Gospel is one of welcome and redemption, and people are starving for that truth. So, if we have a message people actually want to hear, how to we go about delivering it?

This passage emphasizes the power of relationships to heal and reconcile within the church and in the world. It starts with relationship with God, who provides the Spirit of adoption that liberates us from slavery to the flesh. Then it continues on to say that the creation longs for the revealing of the children of God so that they, too, can be set free from bondage. The freedom of the children of God is what reveals God's glory, the glory that the creation groans for. If we are to live this truth today, we cannot be successful by staying within our church walls. The people who need the love and welcoming that the Gospel provides need us to leave our church buildings and to go out and meet them. If God's Spirit is given to us through relationship, then relationships with others are what heal our divisions. If we connect with people in our daily lives at work, at the hair salon, at the grocery store, and in our neighborhoods by establishing relationships and friendships, then the hope for redemption that Paul describes in this passage can be shared.

Pastor Gary Leiderbach from One Direction Community Church shares a story of this relationship building and hope sharing with his experiences at a local Waffle House. Four or five mornings a week Pastor Gary ate breakfast at Waffle House and spent time getting to know some of the regulars and the employees. One of the regulars was a man that Pastor Gary called "Chuck." Chuck was typically crude and had no shortage of swear words. He was often in a bad mood and lashed out at the waitresses and other customers. One morning Pastor Gary accidentally sat in Chuck's seat at Waffle House, and Chuck immediately began swearing at him to move. Before Pastor Gary could respond, two waitresses stepped in and demanded that Chuck stop swearing at him because he was a man of God. In fact, they claimed him, saying that Chuck couldn't yell at "their pastor" that way. The waitresses high fived as Chuck turned around and walked out.

Pastor Gary was amazed that these waitresses who had never attended his church, even though he had invited them many times, claimed him as "their pastor." All of these mornings that he had been eating at Waffle House he had spent this special time talking with them, listening to them, getting to know them, praying with them, and offering scripture. This had created a relationship between them. He had given them spiritual counsel while they were working, so they considered him their pastor. And Chuck took notice of this after the incident. A couple months later, Chuck began opening up to Pastor Gary about his guilt from fighting in Vietnam. He felt as if God could never forgive him for what he had done in the war. Pastor Gary now understood that his abrasive behavior came from his guilt, and he promised to pray for Chuck. Just a couple weeks later, Chuck's 31-year-old son was accidentally killed when a gun misfired. Chuck turned to Pastor Gary to come and speak at his son's memorial service, because he and his wife didn't have a connection to any other church. Pastor Gary told them he would be honored to speak and help them in any way he could through this difficult time. After the service he continued to show up to visit Chuck and his wife, often bringing food. In some ways, Pastor Gary had become Chuck's pastor, too. Pastor Gary spent time with local people outside of the church building, establishing relationships. He heard the groan of creation seeking redemption by talking to these people, his new friends, and offered them hope.

One doesn't have to be a pastor to build these types of relationships and to minister to others. *All* of those who are led of the Spirit are children of God. Paul says that the creation waits eagerly and longingly to see the children revealed in God's glory, not just the pastors. Author Barbara Brown Taylor shares a story in her book, *The Preaching Life,* about a recent college graduate who wanted to become ordained. When she asked him why he wanted to be ordained, he didn't seem interested in serving the church or preaching very often or serving a denomination or participating in the sacraments. Instead, he wanted to be able to approach people on the streets who looked like they needed to talk or reach out to people on the bus who seemed to be hurting. He wanted to be able to help people and share his faith but felt like he needed the "right credentials" to do it. Barbara Brown Taylor was shocked to hear this, and in her book, she proclaims, "God help the church if clergy are the only Christians with 'credentials', and God help all those troubled people on the bus if they have to wait for an ordained person to come along before anyone speaks to them." Beloved, your faith, your baptism, your status as a joint heir with Christ are your credentials to make relationships and spread hope to a longing world. The title "child of God" provides us the authority of the Spirit. The title "joint-heir with Christ" holds us in high regard in God's kingdom since we are set next to the Son of God. Those are the most powerful credentials anyone would need to be a messenger of the Gospel.

As we minister, we use our gifts and talents to share the hope of Christ to the whole world, but we aren't the fixers of the broken or redeemers of the seekers. We are the broken and the redeemed who point to the One in Glory who puts us in right relationship. We are the adopted ones who invite siblings to gather into the mighty arms of our Abba, Father. Often, when we do service projects, volunteer work, and mission trips we are seeking to help people by fixing some sort of problem. Whether that's mending a leaky roof or driving people to destinations that they can't reach themselves, or ladling soup into bowls, we want to be doing something that gives us the automatic sensation of progress, of solving some sort of problem. And that's wonderful! We are called to do this work, to use our time, money, and resources to meet the needs of our community; but sometimes we fail to maintain relationships and friendships with the people that we serve. If we don't see ourselves helping or fixing or solving in some sort of obvious way, we don't always see our usefulness. But a loving, caring presence in the lives of others is always useful. When our relationship with God inspires us to have relationships with others, we can truly go beyond serving by participating in reconciliation and growing our adoptive family. Beyond handing out coats to people on the streets in chilly weather, we could learn their names, encourage them to visit church, invite them to have a meal with us, or take a moment to sit down and listen to their stories. A non-judgmental, listening ear, a smile and a hug, a call on someone's birthday, an invitation to a barbecue can be just as important as a mission trip. Service can be a one-time event. We can do good in someone's life and doing good glorifies God when done in God's love. But if we were to enter into a friendship with the people we serve, with the people in our communities, with the people in the local gym, with the people in the public library, with the people through the fast food drive-through, then hearts can be changed, connections can be made, and the glory of God can be revealed.

One devotional I enjoy reading comes from a man named Josh Akers who shares stories that he calls *Mustard Seeds* about his young son, his church, his friends, and his family as he experiences them throughout the week. He takes some time to reflect on these events to examine how God is at work in his life. He shared a story about his church's Memorial Day Ice Cream Social. He and many other congregation members began handing out ice cream but realized that they had more ice cream than they had people. So, Josh and his son walked down Main Street near their church and simply directed people down the sidewalk to their church for a free sundae. When they finished their trek up and down the road, meeting various people and sending them toward the church, they got back to the parking lot to see that the ice cream, the syrup, and the sprinkles had all been wiped out! In years past they had always had too much left over, but this year when they decided to leave the church grounds to go and meet people who were hungry for what the church had to offer, they were able to share and give away all that they had. One of the people he encountered asked why they did this. Josh said that the church wanted the community to know that they would be welcome and that they wanted to show a type of kindness that represented God's kingdom, a kingdom where all are welcome to share in the joy. Josh's church didn't fix any problems, per se, but they offered an opportunity to show kindness and make new relationships, which their community eagerly responded to.

The creation is groaning, longing for the children of God to be revealed. Our relationship with God through our adoption empowers us to make relationships with others. Our relationships offer an opportunity to glorify God and spread hope. If we are willing to leave the church walls and meet people out in our communities, the Spirit will lead us to people who are starving for the love and the redemption that the Gospel offers. We don't need any special credentials or hold a particular office to look into the eyes of our neighbors and offer a listening ear and a shoulder to cry on. Our status as joint-heirs with Christ is the authority we need to create these types of relationships. We don't have to be fixers, but we point to the Holy Redeemer who heals all hurts. We can let our service work be a one-time thing; or we can seize the opportunity to make friends with the people who eagerly show up, longing for a loving community, an adoptive family. Children of God, the creation is groaning. Let us reveal ourselves and reveal the glory of God.

Unity at the Table
1 Corinthians 11:17-28

Now in the following instructions I do not commend you, because when you come together it is not for the better but for the worse. For, to begin with, when you come together as a church, I hear that there are divisions among you; and to some extent I believe it. Indeed, there have to be factions among you, for only so will it become clear who among you are genuine. When you come together, it is not really to eat the Lord's supper. For when the time comes to eat, each of you goes ahead with your own supper, and one goes hungry and another becomes drunk. What! Do you not have homes to eat and drink in? Or do you show contempt for the church of God and humiliate those who have nothing? What should I say to you? Should I commend you? In this matter I do not commend you! For I received from the Lord what I also handed on to you, that the Lord Jesus on the night when he was betrayed took a loaf of bread, and when he had given thanks, he broke it and said, "This is my body that is for you. Do this in remembrance of me." In the same way he took the cup also, after supper, saying, "This cup is the new covenant in my blood. Do this, as often as you drink it, in remembrance of me." For as often as you eat this bread and drink the cup, you proclaim the Lord's death until he comes. Whoever, therefore, eats the bread or drinks the cup of the Lord in an unworthy manner will be answerable for the body and blood of the Lord. Examine yourselves, and only then eat of the bread and drink of the cup.

When I was a little girl, I was taught that if someone did not shout, testify, become emotional, or affirm the preacher with a resounding "amen" during church services then that meant the person probably had a spiritual problem. They might even be ashamed of the Gospel, and they likely needed to repent. I remember looking around during the church service, taking note of who sat quietly with hands folded, especially during altar calls. If ol' Bobby from up the road did not throw his hands up and shout when Barbara Rose fell sobbing to her knees at the altar to recommit her life to Jesus, I knew that I needed to pray for God to send conviction upon him so that he could repent of his sins and worship the Lord like the rest of us. There were strong implications that it was sinful if there was someone in the church who did not conform to the majority of the congregation.

Then in college when I joined the PC(USA), I became accustomed to a congregation that wasn't typically vocally responsive during worship (unless noted in the bulletin.) Early on in my new commitment to the Presbyterian church, my dad, who is a Baptist pastor, came to a PC(USA) worship service to see me perform a monologue for an Easter service. We were only about two minutes into the service, still in the welcome and introduction portion, when he shouted a riveting "AMEN!" that echoed in the stark silence. This happened again and again throughout the entire service. I remember being so embarrassed because I could not deny that this redheaded, pale-skinned man was my father, and I wished he would just be quiet, respect our traditions, and conform to the majority. Later, I had a conversation about this with a friend who was also at this worship service. He actually enjoyed hearing my dad express himself vocally. It didn't disrupt him, rather, he was encouraged by his responses and enjoyed a change of pace that challenged what he was used to. My friend helped me realize that this attitude I had of judging people who worship differently than me is not conducive to worship and unity in the church. The Apostle Paul might say that this expectation I had of everyone conforming to the majority contributes to divisions and factions.

In our scripture passage we see that the church in Corinth is facing serious divisions and disorders. The people of the church who are disadvantaged are not truly being welcomed to the table, which prohibits unity. Paul says that the people who gather do not "really eat the Lord's Supper" because the people of the congregation "go ahead with their own supper" and "become drunk" while others who do not have provisions of their own are "humiliated." Those who can provide food for the meal gorge themselves, while those who have less to offer are left to sit and watch. Everyone sits together at the table, but there is no sharing among them. Paul says that this "shows contempt for the church of God." Only those who already have an abundance are welcomed to the table and are allowed to participate. The people who cannot conform to the majority, who have less, who are hungry, and who are struggling are the ones who are excluded. This begs the question for our churches today: When we invite people to come worship God with us, what do we do if they take our offer seriously and really show up? Do we leave space for people to worship God in whatever way best expresses their hearts and cultures? Do we expect those who are hungry or those who are addicted or those who are oppressed to leave their struggles outside the church building so that we don't have to see their pain? Do we accommodate all physical and mental abilities or expect them to keep up with pre-established practices? When we say come to the table, do we actually intend to share it with people who are different from us? Or do we hope that they find another table for them to sit at, so that they don't bother us?

I attended a conference called "Disgraced" which addressed the issue of racism in our churches. I participated in a workshop led by Marcia Mount-Shoop who discussed the Eucharist as a healing practice. She told us a story about a small

Presbyterian church, where only white people attended, that wanted to reach out into their community to bring some life into their worship service. The Presbyterian congregation invited a local historically black congregation to come worship and partake in communion with them. The visiting congregation was also invited to lead the musical portions of worship. The Presbyterian congregation didn't expect the clapping, shouting, and tambourine playing to be part of their musical experience. The visiting congregation continued their joyful musical leadership during communion, which was typically a quiet, meditative time for the Presbyterian congregation. This was a new experience for the majority of the people in the hosting congregation. While there were several who were receptive to this new-to-them worship experience, there were many who felt disrupted. One congregation member approached the pastor after the service and said that he didn't mind having the visitors in worship, but that they needed to take communion the "right way." Marcia Mount-Shoop said that in this case unity was being equated with "whiteness."

In the Church of Corinth unity was being equated with affluence. The table should be a place of sharing, celebrating, hurting, and healing. But the table cannot serve this purpose unless this idea of unity being synonymous with conformity is shattered. Only then can we truly be one with one another. Marcia Mount-Shoop explained in our workshop that bringing our authentic selves to the table and laying our vulnerabilities and brokenness down before us is what will bring healing and unity. Healing cannot occur unless the brokenness is exposed. Christ's table centers on brokenness, and it is the perfect place to lay down all that is fragmented. In our scripture passage Paul reiterates the actions of Jesus on the night that the Lord's Supper was instituted. He says that Jesus took a loaf of bread and after giving thanks, he broke it, saying, "This is my body." And Jesus took the cup after supper saying, "This cup is the new covenant sealed in my blood." Central to the Eucharist is the image of a vulnerable, broken body as symbolized by the elements. Paul says each time the supper is eaten the Corinthians are proclaiming the Lord's death. Eating at the table, grabbing the bread, ripping it in two, tearing it to pieces, smearing it in the wine, and grinding it all between teeth is an act of remembrance. Death, being the ultimate form of brokenness, is remembered each time the church gathers to celebrate the Lord's Supper. And in order to partake, Paul says that the Corinthians must examine themselves first. Authenticity, self-reflection, and acknowledging what is broken is the key to finding healing in Christ at the table.

The table invites all people to bring their entire selves, but *we* bear the burden of welcome. We must acknowledge the brokenness inside of us while proclaiming the brokenness that is the foundation of the Lord's Supper so that we might be healed. When we invite others to worship with us, we must be prepared for them to show up and bring everything that makes them unique. This is true unity, not a false unity that is equated to conformity with the majority. We must sit side by side, look each other in the eye, break and share Christ's body, and know our neighbor intimately. There's only one table, but there's plenty of room for all of God's children with plates, cups, bowls, platters, and casserole dishes abundant with love. I invite you to practice communion in whatever manner is most dear to you. Whether that means starting a conversation with a friend, shedding tears, bowing your head in prayer, or shouting and clapping, your authenticity is welcome. I also invite you to be receptive to your neighbor's authenticity. Let's share the table in Eucharistic unity so that we may truly proclaim the Lord's death until he comes.

A Prayer to Share
Ephesians 3:14-21

For this reason I bow my knees before the Father, from whom every family in heaven and on earth takes its name. I pray that, according to the riches of his glory, he may grant that you may be strengthened in your inner being with power through his Spirit, and that Christ may dwell in your hearts through faith, as you are being rooted and grounded in love. I pray that you may have the power to comprehend, with all the saints, what is the breadth and length and height and depth, and to know the love of Christ that surpasses knowledge, so that you may be filled with all the fullness of God. Now to him who by the power at work within us is able to accomplish abundantly far more than all we can ask or imagine, to him be glory in the church and in Christ Jesus to all generations, forever and ever. Amen.

Often when we pray, we struggle to find the words we'd like to pray to God and for others. Sometimes we default to the Lord's prayer or we'll recite a familiar psalm. Sometimes all we can utter is a single word as a prayer. These are all sufficient ways of communing with God. If we are seeking new words to guide us when we pray, we find that scripture is full of prayers, songs, praises, and conversations with God to help guide us when we are searching for ways to speak with God. I want to lift up this scripture as a prayer to use to pray for loved ones when you need some special and encouraging words. In this letter addressed to the saints in Ephesus noted as a writing from Paul, we see that there is emphasis on unity, living a new life, and putting on the armor of God. This letter is believed to have the most comprehensive and cohesive portrait of God's plan, using words to paint a picture of a God who is the ruler of the whole universe with a deep love and wide sovereignty for all of creation. This prayer that we just read truly grasps the expansiveness of the God of the cosmos. So now I use this prayer as my own. This is my prayer for this church so that you will have it prayed for you and you will understand the power of these words. It is important for the church to know that the pastor prays for them. I hope you receive this prayer as a gift and that you will share it with those in your life that you love.

"I pray that, according to the riches of his glory, he may grant that you may be strengthened in your inner being with power through his Spirit, and that Christ may dwell in your heart by faith as you are being rooted and grounded in love." There is a deep richness in this portion of the prayer. This is a powerful blessing to enrich the soul. It is a call for strengthening of the inner being with power through the Spirit. Strengthening our outer being involves good nutrition, exercise, hygiene practices, healthcare, and rest; but strengthening our inner being often involves prayer, care from others, and fellowship. When one being suffers, the other tends to suffer as well. We must take care of ourselves inside and out so that we may be sturdy individuals and a stable team united in the Holy Spirit. In her book *Accidental Saints* Reverend Nadia Bolz-Weber, founder of the church House for All Sinners and Saints, discusses having an experience of strengthening her inner and outer being. She was preparing for a church event while struggling with a back spasm. Nadia had to load and unload her car full of food, spent hours setting everything up, and had to lead worship all while in pain. When much fewer people showed up for the event than she expected, she found herself in a bitter mood, which was only made worse when she found herself cleaning up all alone while others sat around talking and laughing together. One of the congregation members approached her, knowing she was having a rough day, and asked to pray with her. He gathered a small group and they prayed together. Nadia's back spasm released, and the group helped her finished cleaning. This blessing strengthened her outer being by relieving her pain, but also strengthened her inner being by having compassion shown toward her, being prayed over, and having help to clean up. The Holy Spirit is at work among us, and that is so evident when we show up for one another and strengthen each other's inner being. According to the prayer, we do this by being rooted and grounded in love. Author Dianna Butler Bass describes being rooted and grounded by looking for God around us. She explains how churches have tall ceilings and architecture that points up to heaven, but she reminds us not to be so distracted with looking up and having a vertical faith practice, that we forget that God is with us, in each of us, and among us as we walk the earth. Our faith must be horizontal as well. This is how we stay rooted and grounded in love and this is what I pray for us, as we strengthen one another.

"I pray that you have the power to comprehend, with all the saints, what is the breadth, and the length, and the height, and the depth, and to know the love of Christ that surpasses all knowledge, so that you may be filled with all the fullness of God." What a thing to pray for: to comprehend each direction, every corner of the love of Jesus. What a blessing to wish upon someone, to be filled with the fullness of God. Even as I pray this for each of you, I myself don't have a complete understanding of this expansive love and brimming fullness. The closest I have come to having this prayed over me and understanding what it even means was during my time in South Korea with a group from my seminary. After flying to the other side of the world and passing into a time zone that is 14 hours ahead of us, I was greeted with kindness, warmth, love, and hospitality by each person I met while in South Korea. Traveling this far away over a 14-hour period and being met with welcome truly affirmed a comprehension of breadth and length and height and depth of Christ's love.

While we were there our seminary group attended a weekly prayer service held at one of the Korean churches. This prayer service used a type of practice called "tong sung kido." This is a spontaneous prayer spoken out loud; it is not a prayer spoken in tongues, but instead each person prayers out loud their own prayer to God in the Korean language. The pastor would stand before the congregation and discuss an important topic, such as sharing about some of the sick congregation members. Then the entire congregation would cry out to God in unison together, which roughly translates as, "Please God!" and then they would each pray their own prayer out loud on behalf of the sick congregation members. After a period of time the prayer would die down and the pastor would talk about another topic, maybe about their missionaries. Then they would go on into prayer again out loud for the missionaries, and it would continue in this cycle. While we couldn't understand the words that were being spoken, we could feel the passion and intensity behind these prayers. We were surprised when the pastor asked our group to stand up. We were traveling strangers, a group of foreigners, in this church, but he told the congregation that we were seminary students from the United States and that they should pray for us. Then this congregation cried out, "Please God!" They all prayed out loud for us. They cried out with the same passion and intensity as before, on our behalf. To hear voices being uplifted in another language by people who didn't even know us was an experience so profoundly moving, that I will never forget it. This is the closest to the fullness of God I have ever felt, to be overwhelmed by hospitality, love, and prayer by complete strangers to us foreigners, and this is what I pray for each of you.

Our scripture passage ends with a charge and a blessing to the saints of Ephesus, which I also offer as a charge to you, to us as a team: "Now to him who by the power at work within us is able to accomplish abundantly far more than all we can ask or imagine, to him be the glory in the church and in Christ Jesus to all generations forever." Whatever you or I can imagine us accomplishing through love in the name of Jesus is nothing compared to what God can do within us. The potential of this world-changing power is unfathomable and is the blessing I hope for us. Doing the unimaginable will look different from person to person, depending upon our gifts and passion given to us by the Spirit. For example, this might look like a 102 year-old-man who has logged over a thousand hours of service and traveled thousands of miles to volunteer his time to Meals on Wheels. USA Today reports on Edward Kydd in Rockledge, FL, who is not letting his age slow him down. He wants to spend his time giving to others who might need a hot meal brought to their home. Another example of doing the unimaginable might look like New York Daily News' report on English teacher Bijoun Eric Jordan raising over $50,000 to take his students overseas to Japan. Mr. Jordan teaches at a school in Brooklyn where many of his students, who are mostly people of color, come from economically disadvantaged families and neighborhoods. Mr. Jordan knows his students struggle with poverty and are exposed to crime, and he wants them to see the world so that they know there is more out there than what they may be experiencing now. He believes offering them the opportunity to travel to Japan and other countries can be life-changing for these students who may not otherwise be able to afford to see much of the world outside of their neighborhoods. Like Bijoun Eric Jordan and Edward Kydd, if we use our love for others God can accomplish so much more than we could imagine in the world.

Now as this prayer closes, it is yours to hold in your heart and yours to pray over your loved ones. While I pray this for you and for us, I hope you'll join me in this prayer for our church and for our community, too. I believe that if we strengthen one another, remain rooted and grounded, and be open to the fullness of God then the work will be good and beyond all that we can imagine. If we are sharing this prayer as our mission together, raising our voices as one body with this scripture passage as our vision then the power of the Holy Spirit will be a palpable presence. This prayer not only connects us as a church but connects us to our ancestors of the church in Ephesus. Let us pray and enact this together so that God will be glorified in the church for all generations.

Gentleness Born of Wisdom
James 3:5-13

So also the tongue is a small member, yet it boasts of great exploits. How great a forest is set ablaze by a small fire! And the tongue is a fire. The tongue is placed among our members as a world of iniquity; it stains the whole body, sets on fire the cycle of nature, and is itself set on fire by hell. For every species of beast and bird, of reptile and sea creature, can be tamed and has been tamed by the human species, but no one can tame the tongue—a restless evil, full of deadly poison. With it we bless the Lord and Father, and with it we curse those who are made in the likeness of God. From the same mouth come blessing and cursing. My brothers and sisters, this ought not to be so. Does a spring pour forth from the same opening both fresh and brackish water? Can a fig tree, my brothers and sisters, yield olives, or a grapevine figs? No more can salt water yield fresh. Who is wise and understanding among you? Show by your good life that your works are done with gentleness born of wisdom.

These are some harsh words that James chooses to describe the use of our tongues. The tongue is a fire, world of iniquity, it stains the whole body, sets fire to the whole cycle of nature, set on fire by hell, can't be tamed, is a restless evil, full of deadly poison, and used to curse others. It's easy to look at this imagery and think it's a bit dramatic or a little too severe, but James' letter is addressed to the twelve tribes of the Dispersion, which was the description commonly used for Jews scattered outside of Palestine, and this faith community consistently oppressed the poor. They were showing favoritism to the rich, which stood in opposition to the message of the Gospel. We may be tempted to think that such a tongue-lashing was meant for a different audience or is just overdone, but when we live by phrases such as "never discuss religion or politics at the table" or "I'm not opinionated, just always right" or "a closed mouth gathers no foot", then one may realize just how accurate and applicable these descriptions can be. We all have our opinions, which help shape our beliefs and personalities, and they create a beautiful world of diversity. We hold these opinions because we believe they are the right ones. And when we feel as if we are right, especially in American culture, we lavish in our right of "freedom of speech" to ensure each and every person we encounter is well educated on our thoughts on church, war, marriage, and the economy.

One would think this would lead to rich and lively discourse of mutual learning, which would make sharing our own personal views a healthy practice. But in many instances, we have fooled ourselves into thinking that if someone disagrees with us, not only are they wrong, but it is also a personal attack. When we feel attacked, we strike back and use our tongues to create burning words that assert our opinion and scorch those on the receiving end. As a result, we are screaming at the top of our throats about voting red or voting blue or voting somewhere in between, using our words to tear down and destroy one another with the deadly poison dripping from our tongues. Our mouths spew blessing and cursing when we cry out for God to bless America, but secretly hope in the back of our minds that God blesses only those Americans who think like us. We are sources of blessing and cursing if we pray for God to restore our churches, but secretly hope for the demise of the congregation nearby that teaches and preaches differently. We can be quick to forget that the liberal, the conservative, the Muslim, and the atheist were also made in the likeness of God, and do not deserve to be consumed by the fires of our angry tongues. Disagreements among Christians and all other people on earth are bound to happen; it's up to us to prevent these disagreements from staining the whole body of humanity.

This type of fire is a force of destruction, and we are a people who believe in new life, as brought by Jesus. How are we to extinguish the fires we have set ablaze so that healing may occur? James says that our good life can be shown by gentleness born of wisdom. To give birth is to bring new life in the world, and James calls us to birth new life through the waters of gentleness. In his devotional book, *My Utmost for His Highest*, Oswald chambers says, "Always measure your life solely by the standards of Jesus… it takes God a long time to get us to stop thinking that unless everyone sees things exactly as we do, they must be wrong. That is never God's view… Don't get impatient with others. Remember how God dealt with you-with patience and gentleness. But never water down the truth of God." When we are preaching our opinions instead of the Gospel, then what we are communicating is ego instead of truth. If we are projecting our ideals onto other people and allowing them to eclipse our desire to seek justice and reconciliation in the world, then our own opinions have become the authority of our life, rather than Christ.

James comments twice on how small the tongue is. If such a small member of the body cannot be tamed, then maybe a piece of ourselves that is so small can be soothed by acting in gentleness. We might choose to silence our tongues so that the Gospel may be lived and preached by deed. Gentleness is the river that rushes to calm the wildfires and floods our hearts with compassion to feed those who stomach's growl at night, to dig wells for those who lack access to clean drinking water, and to put roofs over the heads of those exposed to the elements. We can let our hands heal what our words have marred; we can yield fresh water to nourish everyone in the light of Christ instead of choking them with brackish water. As we humble ourselves to serve each person, we must take special care to acknowledge the likeness of God appearing in everyone. Perhaps then we can realize our service, our worship, our prayer, our communities, and our fellowship isn't even remotely about us, but about promoting the goodness that unites us in God's love. In a world that revolves around self, ego, and pride, this is a radical message. If we remember that when we walk into our church buildings or when we go on our mission trips that it's not about our own self-gratification, but about seeking what is good then maybe our tongues of fire won't be tamed but quenched.

Should we allow the gifts of our talents and service to speak for us, then perhaps divine gentleness can soothe the fires. I have witnessed this firsthand: As a child growing up in a strict household ruled under the hand of a minister father who often struggled with his temper, my relationship with my Dad was a complicated one. However, he continually sought to become more patient and allowed gentleness to flow when he was teaching my sister and me the things that mattered most to him. As children, each night he would say prayers with us, sing "Jesus Loves Me", and teach us new Bible verses to memorize. He is also is an outdoor enthusiast and taught us how to fish, showing us how to bait our hooks, cast our lines, and reel in a biting catch. These moments of gentleness are what stuck with me as I grew older and are the memories my dad and I reminisce on when we are together.

However, this gentleness does not come as naturally to us as fiery tongues. James asks, who is wise and understanding among you? He says that this gentleness must be birthed from wisdom. This means that the church must seek wisdom in order to nourish our spirits that are pregnant with gentleness.

In order for the church body to grow and stretch to accommodate the developing gentleness, we must cultivate understanding. It takes time for us to grow our knowledge of the world, learn from our mistakes, and allow it to develop into wisdom. In her book *Biblical Womanhood*, author Rachel Held Evans has experience in taking time to birth gentleness and attempting to quench her tongue of fire. She spends a year of her life taking all biblical commandments prescribed explicitly for women as literally as possible. Her first month of this venture is spent specifically on cultivating a quiet and gentle spirit. In order to control her tongue, she keeps a jar of contention where she sheepishly collects coins whenever she complains, gossips, or swears. She begins practicing centering prayers to quiet her thoughts. She does penance by sitting on the roof of her home as a public act of repentance for her rebellious spirit, which, oddly enough, gains unfavorable attention from neighbors and the mail carrier. She even takes an etiquette lesson, where she learned how to eat and act properly in a southern genteel manner at fancy dinner parties. Through this month of experiences, Rachel was able to gain some wisdom on the virtue of gentleness. She sums up the chapter by saying, "Far from connoting timidity or docility, gentleness is associated with integrity and self-control... It forced me to confront some of my uglier tendencies... I found myself reacting less and listening more. I held back, chose my words more carefully, and protected people's reputations by avoiding gossip. The change wasn't dramatic, but I started handling others with just a little more gentleness, a little more care, keeping in mind that we all have fragile days from time to time." Rachel had listened to the wisdom of others and practiced it for herself. This taught her to see the cooling, quelling power of gentleness.

Birthing a gentle spirit from wisdom is a labor of dedicated love, and labor is one of the most self-sacrificing acts a person can perform. When we have taken time to gather wisdom and understand the power of a gentle spirit, then gentleness can be delivered from the church into the world and douse the flames burning the whole cycle of nature. This new creation will not come screaming into the world like most of us do but will come in a cooling quiet pouring out a healing so mighty that only God can provide. The labor pain of change that the church must endure allows our good lives to be shown by our works. Let us set aside our self-gratifying hellfire tongues, so that we are Christ-like servants living our beliefs into existence. Stand proudly by who you are and what you believe, but also be familiar with diversity so that it does seem so threatening. We may not be able to tame our fiery tongues, but we can quench them with divine gentleness.

Now and Yet
1 John 3:1-7

See what love the Father has given us, that we should be called children of God; and that is what we are. The reason the world does not know us is that it did not know him. Beloved, we are God's children now; what we will be has not yet been revealed. What we do know is this: when he is revealed, we will be like him, for we will see him as he is. And all who have this hope in him purify themselves, just as he is pure. Everyone who commits sin is guilty of lawlessness; sin is lawlessness. You know that he was revealed to take away sins, and in him there is no sin. No one who abides in him sins; no one who sins has either seen him or known him. Little children, let no one deceive you. Everyone who does what is right is righteous, just as he is righteous.

This scripture text is an appropriate one for transitions. In a time when the future of our church seems uncertain, as people are leaving the church and moving away, when young families aren't flocking to our congregations, and when pastors move from a congregation leaving everyone a little lost and confused, we might find ourselves out of sorts and wondering where God is in the midst of this mess. Perhaps we feel like our identity as a church is in question, or we might feel like we can't move forward into the unknown. We might feel stuck or inadequate. But the good news that is proclaimed in this letter is that all of these doubts and fears, while valid, are nothing compared to the life of Christ that is within us right now, here in this transitional moment. Even when it feels like we've lost our footing, God's grace is still sufficient, and the Holy Spirit is still at work within us and around us.

The church that John is addressing has lost members whose beliefs no longer aligned with that of the church. When people leave the church all parties often harbor pain of some sort, and this can leave the future of the church shaky. Growing up in my faith tradition, I went through numerous church splits; sometimes we were the ones who left, and other times we were the ones who stayed. I experienced my first church split at four years old. There were years after this first schism when the name of the church was spoken only in anger, and certain names of people who had once been friends now carried painful baggage. That was the first of several church splits I endured, and each one evoked an emotional response that took years to heal from. When the church community is full of someone's closest friends and family, any sort of break in the congregation can feel like the world is crumbling. John is doing his pastoral duty by caring for this congregation who is facing emotional turmoil. The burden has fallen to him to give them something to hold onto and be assured of. This letter addresses who the church is right now in the midst of this chaos: right now, they are children of God. Nothing can change that. God's claim on their lives is sufficient. The passage also discusses what they are all waiting for, what is yet to come: God's revelation. One day God will be revealed, and the future of the church will be revealed. It's not happening just yet, but the church can rely on God's promise of kingdom come. God's grace is more than enough for the present and the future of the church, and John is inviting them to lean into this for comfort and to sustain their faith. God is here in the now and is also the God of yet to come.

The bold declaration from this scripture that says, "Beloved, we are God's children now" is a grounding statement that reminds us of who we are and whose we are. John wants the church to be assured of their identity, an infallible truth that will not be taken away from them. We can share in John's reminder to the congregation that our identity in Christ as God's children is an unshakeable fact when the world seems to pitch beneath our feet. When it feels like everything in our lives is changing, being God's child is the one unchangeable truth that we can rely on. John wrote this to help steady the church and remind them that who they are right now in this moment is still the church following Jesus' mission. They are still fully equipped to do this, no matter who comes and who goes within the church. We, as the church that we are right now, have the gifts and abilities to be effective ministers of the Gospel of Jesus Christ. John reminded this church of their mission to strive for purity, sinlessness, and righteousness. This is their mission, and they are still fully equipped to fulfill their ministry as a church. When we think of our mission to love with pure hearts, to flee from sin, and to seek justice and righteousness, we need not fear that God has left us without the ability to follow through as faithfully as possible.

Author Joan Gray writes in her book *Sailboat Church* about how churches, no matter how large or how small, are bursting with the gifts and talents that they need to be a powerful force of the Holy Spirit within their communities. It's about recognizing and using the strengths of the congregation instead of forcing projects, ministries, and missions that the church may not be equipped for. She asks us to imagine a church full of people who have the gifts for teaching: maybe their ministries would be best focused on after school programs or Bible studies for a prison outreach. Then we are asked to imagine a church that has a strong congregational focus on prayer; perhaps they might serve their community best through intercession and healing. Joan then asks the reader to imagine a church that is full of people who are gifted with hospitality; maybe their gifts could provide sponsorship programs for refugees. The possibilities are endless! Instead of a church trying to do too much, or trying to be everything to everyone, a congregation is strongest when it recognizes the strengths already in their pews and they use those specific skills to serve the community in a focused way. Joan wants her readers to know that regardless of what they hope their church might become in the future, that the church members they have now are talented and able to follow the guidance of the Holy Spirit to be a mighty blessing. John wants his readers to know this too; who they are right now is enough to be a blessing. No matter what changes come our way, we as the church need not fear a lack of skills, gifts, and abilities. So long as a congregation exists, the Holy Spirit is pouring out blessings over God's people offering guidance, opportunities, skills, and growth. All we have to do is open our eyes to the work that the Spirit is already doing among us, and then we actively join in.

John also reminds the reader that the best is yet to come. He does not call them to look forward for their identity; he wants them to be stable and confident in their congregation now. However, the pain, the conflict, the disagreements will all one day pass away when Jesus comes again, and God's glory is fully revealed. As I stated before, I went through several church splits in my life. It always felt like the end of the world in many ways. As a child it was difficult for me to grasp why adults would get into disagreements that were bad enough to tear a church apart. The people that I had grown to love and trust in my faith community were no longer going to be in my life. Old friendships often fell apart, and this left deep wounds. However, we were able to walk through this pain by joining together with other people who were hurting so that we might weep, pray, and grieve together. As an adult, I now look back and realize that many of these painful experiences were not always handled in the healthiest way. But I also see that there was always a way to find hope. We formed new faith communities, relying on our belief in Jesus Christ to overcome the pain. We placed our faith in the eternal love of God, trusting that God would be revealed in glory, and that the pain and suffering we endured was temporary. John understands that his readers may be losing friendships, and that this transition may feel like the end of the world. Their Christian community as they know it is changing, but John wants to remind them that God has yet to reveal the glorious future that is to come.

Author JRR Tolkien expresses the hope of the future, hope that the best is yet to come, in his book *The Return of the King* which is the final book in *The Lord of the Rings* trilogy. In these books there is a ring of power that an evil spirit, known as Sauron, is bound to. If Sauron gets the ring, he will have the ultimate power over this world, known as Middle Earth; so, the ring must be destroyed. There are wizards, dwarves, humans, elves, hobbits (who are like humans, but much shorter in stature), and many other mythical creatures who are fighting over the ring. Our main characters, Frodo and Sam who are hobbits, are the pair who everyone is relying on to make sure the ring is thrown into the fire of Mount Doom. Frodo and Sam risked their lives to complete this task, knowing that they would likely die in the process and believing that most of their friends would die as well. Every city and kingdom have joined in the fight; most cities are fighting for their lives against the armies of Sauron. It truly feels like the end of the world and that evil might win. However, the unlikely heroes narrowly succeed, and the ring is destroyed. Frodo and Sam collapse, and although they triumphed in their mission it seems like this may be the end for them. The hobbits are surprised when they awaken to find themselves safe and being watched over by their wizard friend, Gandalf. Sam has hope in the immediate future, that now that the evil is gone that the best is yet to come. He asks Gandalf, "Is everything sad going to come untrue? What's happened to the world?" Gandalf responds that a great shadow has departed, and then they are all able to laugh together in pure bliss and merriment. Now that the evil had passed away, there was hope for a brighter future and a happier life. Just as the people of Middle Earth could have hope that evil would no longer prevail and that there is hope in what is yet to come, John wants to remind his readers that there is hope for tomorrow even if it feels like the end of the world. We, as the church, need not fear change or endings because the pain that these things bring will pass away when God reveals the glorious yet to be.

John reassures his readers, known as little children, with fatherly kindness by reminding them of the now and that of yet. They are the children of God right now in this moment; they are still fully equipped and completely capable to enact the ministry of Jesus Christ. And yet, God will be revealed, and they will be like God. When we go through changes and transitions, our pain, fear, and anger are valid; however, this does not mean that all is lost. When people leave the church, when pastors come and go, when the church doesn't show signs of growth, let us not be fooled into thinking that the Holy Spirit is finished with us. Who we are right now in Jesus Christ is more than enough to be powerful witnesses to the Gospel in the world, and we can live into the hope that our suffering will pass away because the best is yet to come. Take heart that all believers since the very beginning of the church have weathered transitions and changes, and yet the church of Jesus Christ has persisted and prevailed. Let us celebrate who we are now, rejoicing in the hope of yet.

www.ingramcontent.com/pod-product-compliance
Lightning Source LLC
Chambersburg PA
CBHW052149110526
44591CB00012B/1915